Pass the QTS Skills Tests with Con

G000057346

Pass the QTS Skills Tests with Confide
prospective trainee teachers. It will pro
subject knowledge and confidence you need to pass the Literacy and
Numeracy QTS Skills Tests, make an application that stands out and sail
through interview day.

The first section of the book introduces you to the tests and how to
prepare for them, and covers the areas of knowledge tested. The second
section offers advice to help you write a personal statement that stands
out, make a successful application and get ready for your interview.
Extensive online support provided on the companion website includes
tests to audit your subject knowledge.

Key topics covered include:

- developing your exam technique
- mastering the mental arithmetic test
- succeeding in the written questions
- how to use spelling, grammar and punctuation correctly
- successfully applying for teacher training courses
- acing the interview.

Written by expert teacher trainers with first-hand experience of both
interviewing candidates and helping students pass the QTS Skills Tests,
this is an essential purchase for all prospective teachers.

Tony Cotton is a writer and educational consultant. Previously he has been
Head of the School of Education and Childhood at Leeds Metropolitan
University, UK, Programme Leader for the BA Primary Education at
Nottingham Trent University, UK, and Course Leader for the PGCE
Mathematics at Nottingham University, UK.

Dave Klemm has experience as Head of English across a range of
secondary schools in Yorkshire. He has carried out many Ofsted
inspections and worked at Leeds University, UK, on the PGCE Secondary
English.

Pass the QTS Skills Tests with Confidence

And ace your interview

Tony Cotton and Dave Klemm

Routledge
Taylor & Francis Group

LONDON AND NEW YORK

First published 2016
by Routledge
2 Park Square, Milton Park, Abingdon, Oxon OX14 4RN

and by Routledge
711 Third Avenue, New York, NY 10017

Routledge is an imprint of the Taylor & Francis Group, an informa business

© 2016 T. Cotton and D. Klemm

British Library Cataloguing in Publication Data
A catalogue record for this book is available from the British Library

Library of Congress Cataloging-in-Publication Data
Cotton, Tony.
  Pass the QTS skills tests with confidence : and ace your interview /
Tony Cotton and Dave Klemm.
  pages cm
  1. Teachers – Certification – Great Britain. 2. Educational tests and
measurements – Great Britain – Study guides. 3. Teaching –
Standards – Great Britain. 4. Teachers – Training of – Great Britain.
I. Klemm, Dave. II. Title.
  LB1773.G7C67 2015
  371.120760942 – dc23
  2014049460

ISBN: 978-1-138-81040-2 (hbk)
ISBN: 978-1-138-81041-9 (pbk)
ISBN: 978-1-315-70998-7 (ebk)

Typeset in Celeste and Optima
by Florence Production Ltd, Stoodleigh, Devon, UK

MIX
Paper from
responsible sources
FSC
www.fsc.org   FSC® C013604   Printed and bound by CPI Group (UK) Ltd, Croydon, CR0 4YY

Contents

Contents

Contents

Acknowledgements

Tony would like to thank all those he has interviewed for teacher training programmes. He has gained his experience from the often fascinating discussions he has had with them. He would also like to thank the many people he has worked with on developing their confidence in mathematics. It is through working with them that he has learned how to become more effective himself. Finally, as always, he sends thanks to Helen for proof reading, asking the right questions and telling him when he gets it wrong. She also tried the numeracy sections out as a learner – even taking practice tests. The book is much better for her input.

Dave would like to thank all the students who have been such an inspiration to him over the last few years. The future of the profession is in very good hands. They have taught him more than they could ever realise. His thanks go to Mary, who has patiently supported him and advised him on writing the text. As ever, her comments have been constructive and apposite.

1 Why do I have to take the skills tests?

The QTS Skills Tests

If you have bought this book, or had this book bought for you, then you must have decided to become a teacher. Well done – and what a great choice of career! A friend once said to me that being a teacher was the second most important job in the world. Midwives have the most important job because they bring babies into the world. Teachers come next because they prepare us all to make our own way in the world.

But, before you can be accepted onto your teacher training course and start that exciting journey, you must pass skills tests in numeracy and literacy. You may be worried about this; you may not be sure why you need to take another test because you will have already passed your GCSEs in English and mathematics. This book is designed to stop you worrying and to help you pass the tests with absolute confidence.

You would probably agree that all teachers, whatever their subject background and whatever the subject they teach, must be able to model good practice in English and mathematics. This is particularly true of primary school teachers, but all secondary teachers should be encouraging literacy through their subject and should be able to make cross-curricular links with mathematics. All teachers will need to be able to write effectively as a part of their

Why do I have to take the skills tests?

professional role and will need to be able to understand and use data to assess the effectiveness of their teaching.

If you think about it, you will be marking books, writing reports and letters that will be sent home to parents, and writing resources to support your teaching. All of these activities require a good level of literacy skills. There is nothing worse than receiving a badly written report on your child and your pupils will delight in picking you up on any literacy errors you make in your resources or presentations.

Similarly you will be asked to use numeracy skills to examine assessment data about the pupils you teach. Having good numeracy skills also allows you to take control of things like timetables and budgets.

Perhaps most importantly, teachers who are confident in both literacy and mathematics make excellent role models for the pupils they teach. We don't want teachers who are scared of mathematics teaching us, do we? If all teachers enjoyed literacy and mathematics and relished the lessons in which they could show off their skills in these areas, schools would be much better places.

So, the tests are designed to cover the core skills that you will need to be a teacher, whether or not you have a specialism in literacy or numeracy. They do not replace the GCSE grade C equivalence, rather they test your understanding of the literacy and numeracy skills that you are likely to need on a day-to-day basis in school. All the questions use real data and information you are likely to come across in school.

The tests are computerised and can be taken in test centres across England. If you have been entitled to reasonable adjustments for any of your examinations before, make sure that you apply to the test centre for special arrangements.

You are allowed two re-sits per subject. If you fail the two re-sits, you have to wait two years until you can try again. So it is really important that you are confident you will be able to pass before you take a test.

How does this book help?

As you read the book, you will be introduced to the structure and content of the skills tests. All the subject knowledge that is tested is explained and there is support through audits and practice questions. These practice questions appear in the same format as they do in the actual tests, so you will get used to the format of the tests.

The book describes the form that the tests take, including the content that will be tested and the way in which the questions will be asked. There is also advice on how best to revise for the tests so that you know when you sit the tests you will be successful. Before reading the chapters that focus on subject knowledge, you should take the online subject knowledge audit. This will allow you to take practice tests in both literacy and numeracy and will support you in putting together an action plan so that you can focus on the areas you need to revise most. There are also sets of practice questions in each of the subject knowledge sections. As you work through these questions, focus on the areas that you find more challenging rather than spending lots of time practising areas that you already feel confident in.

Once you have been successful in passing the tests, the next hurdle is to gain a place on a teacher training course. The final two chapters in this book support you through this process. There are tips that will help you to write an effective personal statement and an online worksheet that you can use to devise a good personal statement. The final chapter gives you advice on how best to prepare for the application day, including planning a presentation and sample questions that can help you prepare for the interview.

You may not feel confident in your own subject knowledge at the moment. This book is designed to give you the confidence to take and pass the tests and to be successful in your application so you can start to become the best teacher you can be.

Who are the authors?

Tony has written the chapters on mathematics. He was a mathematics teacher in primary and secondary schools for 15 years and loved working with other teachers to excite them about teaching mathematics. Since then he has worked for commercial publishers writing resources for pupils both in the UK and internationally. He has also written *Understanding and Teaching Primary Mathematics*, which you will probably use as part of your teacher training when you gain a place on a teacher training course. He worked in universities training teachers for nearly 20 years and in all that time every student he worked with successfully passed the numeracy skills test.

Dave has written the literacy chapters and he has experience as Head of English across a range of secondary schools in Yorkshire. He has also carried out many Ofsted inspections and worked at Leeds University on the Secondary English PGCE. This role included supporting students in passing the English Skills Tests. He designed the 'in-house' tests used by the university in their recruitment and selection process, so is in a great position to help you pass these tests.

Both Dave and Tony have spent many hours reading applications and interviewing for teacher training courses. They will share this experience with you in the later chapters to make sure that you are successful in your application once you have passed the skills tests.

What should I do first?

Read Chapter 2 to find out what the tests look like, then take the online practice tests that you have free access to as a result of buying this book. You will find these tests at www.routledge.com/cw/cotton. These tests will allow you to audit your current subject knowledge in literacy and numeracy. You can now put a revision plan in place so that you are confident you will pass the tests before you book your place at the test centre.

2 | What do the tests look like?

This chapter explains:

- What the tests look like.
- The knowledge you need to pass the skills tests with confidence.
- The practicalities about taking the tests.
- How you can best revise for the tests.

The tests

You take both tests online at one of the test centres nationwide. You answer on-screen questions, some of which are spoken through headphones – for example, the mental arithmetic test and the spelling test. You read other questions on-screen and respond by selecting or typing in answers. Before you start the process of revising for the test and applying to take the test, make sure that you get the most up-to-date information from http://sta.education.gov.uk/.

If you have previously been entitled to additional time or other special arrangements in examinations, you will be able to apply for special arrangements for these tests too.

What do the tests look like?

There are different versions of the tests to cater for different needs. You need to submit evidence to support any request for adaptations, which include:

- 25% and 50% extra time versions
- on-screen spelling questions in literacy tests
- on-screen mental arithmetic questions in numeracy tests
- paper-based tests (including larger print format).

The pass mark for both tests currently is 63%. There are 28 questions in the numeracy test, so you will need to get 17 or 18 correct to pass. There are between 41 and 49 marks available for the literacy test, so you need between 26 and 31 correct to pass this test.

The tests are computer-marked, so you will get your result immediately.

Booking your test

Step 1: Apply for a teacher training course. You will need proof of application when you attend the test centre.

Step 2: Register online at the Department for Education website. This is easy to do. Just go to: http://sta.education.gov.uk/ and follow the on-screen instructions. Make sure the details you provide exactly match those on your application because these will be checked at the test centre. You will be given a 'Skills Tests Account'.

Make sure you use a valid email address. All correspondence about the tests will be sent to this address and you don't want to miss any messages.

In fact it may be a good time to think about creating a new email address that you can use for all professional correspondence. As a teacher you need to ensure that your online profile is professional. Remember pupils and their parents may access any online presence. Make sure there is nothing accessible that could embarrass you. I remember a student of mine who had an email address 'moodycow@ . . .'. This did not create a great first impression.

Step 3: When you are ready, log in to your account and book the tests at a local test centre. Choose a test centre that doesn't involve too much travelling.

Step 4: Attend the test. You need to take a copy of your application form for a teacher training course, the email confirming your test booking and two forms of ID including photo ID such as a passport or driving licence.

The numeracy test

The numeracy skills test covers three areas: mental arithmetic, interpreting and using written data, and solving written arithmetic problems. You have 48 minutes to complete the test. Most of the people who fail the test talk about the difficulty of the pressure of time, so if you have a registered disability that entitles you to special arrangements in examinations make sure that you contact the test centre to get special arrangements granted.

Before you book the test make sure you are confident that you will not feel the pressure of time. I'm afraid that this does come through practice – you will become quicker through practice, so make sure that you time yourself when you are practising questions.

There are 28 questions in each test: 12 mental arithmetic and 16 on-screen. All the questions carry one mark, even though some questions require more than one answer.

Mental arithmetic questions

The Department for Education describes the reason for the mental arithmetic test:

> *the ability to work out answers to straightforward questions which are heard rather than read is an important attribute for*

What do the tests look like?

teachers to possess. Simple mistakes or a lack of speed in mental calculation will often be detected by colleagues, pupils and parents. The ability to calculate mentally in everyday and educational situations is seen as an important aspect of a teacher's professional duties.

You listen to the 12 mental arithmetic questions through headphones and these questions will cover areas such as time, fractions, percentages, measurements and conversions. Each question is read out twice and after the second reading you are given 18 seconds to answer. Once the test moves on from a question, you cannot go back.

You are not allowed to use a calculator, although you can jot down notes on a laminated card with a fine non-permanent marker that is provided by the test centre. You are not allowed to take any notes or support materials in to the test room.

Questions might cover any of the areas below:

Time: Organising timed interviews at a parents' evening.

Money: Converting between currencies in the context of a school trip or about the costs of buying resources.

Proportions: Proportions of boys and girls in your class linked to assessment results or percentage increase and decrease if you are making purchasing decisions.

Fractions, decimals and percentages: Adding, subtracting, multiplying and dividing using fractions, decimals and percentages.

Measurements: Distance and time or lengths, areas or volumes.

As with all the questions, the context will be an everyday context that you may have to deal with in the classroom.

All these areas are covered in the book.

Examples of the questions you might be asked are:

- Teachers organised activities for 4 classes of 27 pupils and 3 classes of 32 pupils. How many pupils were involved altogether?

- A school has a homework policy that pupils should spend 3 hours a week on homework. What is the mean time a pupil would spend on their homework if they do not do any homework on a Saturday or Sunday?

Chapter 4 will give you all the support you need to tackle the mental arithmetic section confidently within the time limit.

Written questions

This section is a series of on-screen questions. For these questions you are provided with an on-screen calculator. There are 16 questions in this section and you could be asked to give the answer in any of the following ways:

- Multiple choice answers, where you pick the correct answer from a range of possibilities.

- Multiple response answers, where you have to choose all possible correct answers from a list of statements.

- Questions that require you to type in a single answer.

- Questions where you will have to 'point and click' on the correct answer.

- Questions where you will have to 'drag and drop' your chosen answer into selected boxes.

Some of the written questions have been designed to test your ability to interpret and use written data in order to:

- identify important trends in data

- make comparisons to draw conclusions that can inform your teaching

- interpret information accurately.

What do the tests look like?

Other questions will ask you to solve written arithmetic problems that test your understanding of:

- time
- money
- proportion and ratio
- percentages, fractions and decimals
- measurements (e.g. distance, area)
- conversions (e.g. from one currency to another, from fractions to decimals or percentages)
- averages (including mean, median, mode and range)
- using simple formulae.

When you answer questions you should follow the advice on the format the answer should take. This advice tells you that when you type numbers into answer boxes you should:

- always give your answer as a number not words
- not add any additional numbers, letters, spaces or symbols or your answer may be marked as incorrect
- not enter any zeros in front of your answer, so enter 21 rather than 021 or 12.5 rather than 012.5
- enter fractions using the 'forward slash' key, so 'one-half' should be entered as 1/2
- enter 24-hour clock times using a colon, for example 2.30 pm should be written as 14:30
- enter decimal numbers using a 'full stop' for the decimal point, for example 12.5
- not type in the units (for example, £, pupils, %) if they are already specified in the question.

The literacy test

The literacy test lasts for 45 minutes and covers spelling, punctuation, grammar and comprehension. As you can imagine, this time will pass quickly so make sure that you have prepared yourself well.

The spelling test is worth 10 marks. You listen to 10 sentences and you are asked to spell one word in that sentence.

The punctuation section is worth 15 marks and contains 15 questions that ask you to insert the correct punctuation.

The grammar section carries between 10 and 12 marks and asks you to select the correct option from a series of choices of text so that a paragraph is grammatically correct.

The comprehension section also carries between 10 and 12 marks, depending on the test. This part of the test asks you to answer comprehension questions about a short piece of text (600–700 words).

The spelling section

The spelling section is an audio test heard through headphones and must be answered first. This is the only part of the test that may not be revisited after you have left it. The words tested are those that you could reasonably be expected to use in your professional role as a teacher; the words are not especially obscure or technical and are used frequently in professional writing. You will not be penalised if you adopt American English when asked to spell a word that has an -ise or -ize suffix, otherwise you are required to use standard British English.

You are given a sentence in which the word you are required to spell could be used. Use this because the context can help you remember how to spell the word. You can listen to the word as many times as you like before typing in your answer. After you have typed your response, read the sentence to yourself to make sure you have used the correct word.

What do the tests look like?

Each word is worth 1 mark, so if you know that you cannot spell a word it is better to leave it out rather than spend a lot of time on one or two words. You can come back to words while you remain in the spelling section of the test, so it is better to complete the ones you are certain about first and then return to any you are unsure of. Remember you only have 45 minutes for the whole test, so you need to be careful how long you spend on each section. Make sure that you use the practice materials so that you are confident this section will not take you too long.

The punctuation section

This section of the test is worth 15 marks and contains 15 questions that require you to insert the correct punctuation. You are not asked to remove or rewrite any sections of the passage that may contain instances where punctuation is acceptable but not essential. If there are examples of nonessential punctuation, you will not gain extra marks or lose any marks.

The grammar section

This section is designed to test your ability to identify text that doesn't follow good grammatical practice. You will need to distinguish between text that makes sense and clearly conveys its intended meaning and text that doesn't by selecting the correct option from a series of options. The test isn't designed to test you on your knowledge of grammatical terms; rather it checks that you can use grammar correctly.

The task may be to put together a letter to parents. In this example you would be asked to select the most appropriate choice for insertion in the letter from several options to complete the letter. There will be four or more points at which you make this choice. There will be between 8 and 12 marks available for this section of the test.

The comprehension section

This section also carries between 8 and 12 marks and asks you to read a short passage of text, usually a passage from the educational press or a government document, and interpret it.

The questions you are asked will test your ability to identify main points in a text, distinguish between facts and opinions, retrieve facts and key points, make inferences and deductions, evaluate meaning and status. Sometimes you will be asked to re-work, organise and structure the information. The knowledge that you will be tested on will include:

- Attributing statements to categories.
- Completing a bulleted list.
- Sequencing information.
- Presenting main points.
- Matching texts to summaries using a multiple-choice tick box.
- Identifying the meaning of words and phrases using a multiple-choice tick box.
- Evaluating statements about the text using a multiple-response letter in box.
- Selecting headings and subheadings using a multiple-choice tick box.
- Identifying possible readership or audience for a text using a multiple-choice letter in a box.

The rest of the book deals in detail with the knowledge that you will need to pass the tests with confidence. We would suggest that you work through the online practice tests available at www. routledge.com/cw/cotton first. The result of this self-audit will allow you to focus on the areas that you most need to work on.

3 How should I prepare for the tests?

This chapter explains:

- The steps you can take to revise effectively.
- Techniques you can use every day to develop your mathematics and literacy skills.

You have already been successful in examinations. In order to get yourself into a position to apply for a teacher education course you will have gained good grades in mathematics and English, and probably many other subjects too. Try to think about the examinations that you entered with confidence. You probably knew what to expect from those examinations and were confident that you had the knowledge that you needed to answer the questions that came up – whatever the questions were.

So take yourself back to the days when you were preparing for these examinations. Treat the Qualified Teacher Status (QTS) Skills Tests in the same way. Enter the test centre feeling confident and prepared. You know you will pass because you know exactly what to expect and are confident that your numeracy and literacy skills will get you through.

Whenever I work on a project (and revising for the skills test is a project), I plan it out. I recommend writing a revision plan. Work backwards from the date you want to take your tests. Block out periods of time that you can spend on study and put these in your diary. Then look though this book and chunk it up. You will know from the initial audit which areas you need to spend more time on and which you can probably skim over. While you will need to be flexible with this plan as your study progresses, crossing the days out as you proceed gives you a sense of progress, which will add to your confidence.

Don't expect to be successful straight away. I was on a train recently and a couple opposite me were discussing the Driving Test theory section. One of the couple said, 'I only got about two right the first time I did the practice test, but after I had done loads of revision I got more and more right.' See the process of revising for these tests in the same way. The first time you take the tests you will probably make lots of mistakes: learn from these mistakes; revisit the areas that you are struggling with. It may take several visits. Eventually you will get there, we promise!

Where should I work?

You already know the answer to this. You know what works for you. Some people work best with music on (as I type this I am listening to Dandelion radio on the internet), some people need silence. I do think that somewhere personal rather than social is helpful. This may be a quiet place in a shared house – a desk in a corner, a desk in a bedroom. It may be a favourite corner of a quiet bar or coffee shop. Some people prefer to cloister themselves away in a library. Try all of these options out and see which works best. You might find you use different places to study at different times. Wherever you choose, make sure that you can make yourself comfortable both in terms of being able to sit for a long period of time without getting sore and in terms of not feeling self-conscious about being there.

How should I prepare for the tests?

Wherever you decide to work, you need to be able to make sure that you can focus completely on the task. Avoid working in places where others will constantly disturb you. You can minimise distractions by putting on earphones (even if you don't listen to music, this stops people disturbing you – honestly, try it).

One thing that may seem contradictory is that I think you should work somewhere where people are available for conversation. You will be able to understand things better if you have to explain them to somebody else. So, ideally, work through this book with a friend or a colleague. Don't talk all the time but take breaks and talk through what you have been looking at with them. Check out your understanding with them. They don't have to be studying for a QTS skills test; a trusted friend or barista can take on this role just the same. I once told my Dad that he was the best teacher I had ever had. I had remembered him sitting down with me to help me with my mathematics A-level homework and explaining it to me much more clearly than my teachers ever had. He told me that he never understood the mathematics, he just asked me to talk through what I had worked on in school until I came to the point at which I had got stuck. Because I had explained my own thinking carefully, I always managed to see the next step even if it hadn't made sense at the time.

Now that you have decided on the space that you are going to work in, you need to put together a set of resources to work with. What toolkit will you take to your place of study?

What resources do I need to prepare myself?

If you haven't done it already, go and treat yourself to two nice notebooks. Label one 'Numeracy QTS Skills Tests' and the other – yes, you're ahead of me – 'Literacy QTS Skills Tests'. I think notebooks are a way of keeping your thoughts neat and tidy – they also act to show you how much you have progressed. I always just write on the left-hand page of a notebook; this leaves the other page for additional notes I add when I flick back through the notebook. Or for notes to myself, such as 'Yes, I understand how to work out percentages now'.

Some of you will find that using colours helps. Design your own keys so that one colour is 'key facts' another is 'practice questions', another is 'things I still don't understand', and so on.

Alternatively you may be like me and prefer to always work in pencil and use boxes or underlining to distinguish different parts of the text. In which case treat yourself to a nice box of pencils with rubbers on the end and a pencil sharpener.

Buy yourself a dictionary and a thesaurus if you don't already have them. These will help you check those spellings you are unsure of and look for alternative words as you develop your writing skills. You will definitely need a calculator; people who learn with calculators actually do better on non-calculator examinations, so use one. It isn't cheating. The dictionary and the calculator can be seen in the same way – they are tools that help you learn how to spell and how to calculate mentally. You can use them to check answers and they will help you become more and more confident that you can get answers correct without needing them.

So:

• Notebooks.

• Pens and pencils.

• Dictionary and thesaurus.

• Calculator.

• Copy of *Passing the Skills Tests with Confidence.*

You have all you need to start studying.

Can I develop my exam technique?

Most of my students say that the hardest thing about the QTS Skills Tests is the pressure of time. This can lead to feelings of tension and students describe the nerves growing as the pressure of time starts to tell.

The most important thing about exam technique is knowing what is coming. Because you will have spent a lot of time looking at questions that follow the same format as those in the tests, there should be no surprises.

You can practice your exam technique by making sure you follow a routine whenever you sit down to study.

- Are you sitting comfortably? Notice how you are sitting. Don't hunch over the keyboard. Sit up straight. Adjust the chair so that you can be comfortable when you are reading the screen. If you have ever seen a concert pianist, you know that they always adjust their piano stool before they start. This is the way they take control of the space and make sure they are ready to give their best performance.

- Don't forget to breathe. Taking two or three deep breaths before you start is another way to take control of the situation. It will calm you down and it will also make sure that you have enough oxygen in your system to operate effectively. If it works for having a baby, surely it will work for taking a test!

- Stay positive. Before you start, remind yourself of all the successes you have had while studying. The great marks in the practice tests. The things you have learnt that you had forgotten or never knew.

Practise these techniques every time you settle down to work; that way they will come naturally when you sit down for the real thing.

Immediately before the test, glance at these notes to remind yourself of what you can do in the test to maximise your marks.

- Read the questions first. If you can, read a section all the way through before you start answering the questions. This is not a waste of time because you will be thinking all the time you are reading. It also allows you to answer the questions that you can answer quickly first. This is a good way of using time efficiently.

- Answer the easy questions first. This is really important in terms of maximising your marks. And as we all know, 'an easy question is one that you know the answer to'!

- If you get stuck on a question, leave it and come back to it. Don't spend a long time on a question that you are struggling with. If you can, mark it with a marker and then come back to it later. You may well discover that answering other questions helps you realise what you need to do on the question that you got stuck on. Those of you who do crosswords know that sometimes answers come to you after a night's sleep. I know we don't have that much time, but moving away from something sometimes allows you to come to a moment of realisation.

- Don't leave blanks. As you reach the end of your time, make sure you have answered every question. You certainly won't get any marks for blank spaces on the answer sheet.

Everyday mathematics and literacy

Of course, you need to keep reminding yourself that you are not simply studying mathematics and literacy to pass the skills tests. There is that functional element to what you will be doing in the next few months, but try to see it as falling back in love with mathematics and literacy as well. Or, maybe, even falling in love with them for the first time.

Here are a range of activities you can do every day to get into the habit of looking at the world in mathematical and literate ways.

Mathematics

Set yourself questions that you want to know the answer to

I look in the newspaper every day to see what mathematics is needed to make sense of the news. For example, I am writing this the day after the closing ceremony for the Commonwealth Games in Glasgow, so the medal table in the newspaper offers me lots of ideas.

I could work out which was the most successful country by finding the medals total as a percentage of the country's population. I could pick countries and draw the gold, silver and bronze medals on a pie chart. I could select the 'home nations' and draw bar charts to allow me to compare the countries.[1]

On most days newspapers offer graphs or tables of information (data) to explain news stories. Examine these in some detail. Ask yourself, are there other ways to represent the data? What facts can you deduce from the data? Starting to look at news in this way helps you become a 'critical mathematician' as well as giving you confidence for the data handling section of the tests. It will also give you lots of ideas in order to bring the real world into your mathematics lessons.

Shopping

There are simple things you can do whenever you go shopping, or to the bar, which will help you develop your mental calculation skills.

As you go round the supermarket, keep a running total of the cost of the items in your head; similarly, try to estimate how much the round will be every time you go to the bar. You can also work out the change that you will be owed. Whenever you eat a meal out together, you be the one who offers to work out how much you should each pay. Not only will your mental maths get better, but your friends will love you even more!

You can set yourself calculations involving percentages. How much would that item be if it was reduced by 10% or 15%? What if I bought four of those tins of tomatoes – how much would that be? Once you get into these habits, you won't be able to stop yourself.

Play with numbers

Every day, pick a 'number of the day' for yourself. Write the number in the middle of a piece of paper and think of all the different facts you know about the number. Work out 50%, 10%, 5% of the numbers and so on. Write down all the calculations that you can think of that have this number as the answer. By playing with numbers in this way you will begin to see numbers as your friend – they will stop being scary and become things that you can literally 'play with'. Whenever you catch a bus, use the bus number; if you are in a car, look at other registration plates and do the same.

A student of mine was telling me recently that whenever she went on long car journeys with her brother, they would use the digital clock to set each other calculations. For example, it is 12:21 as I write this sentence. I am 54 years old. Can you use the digits 1, 2, 2, 1 and any of the operations +, –, ×, ÷ to give the answer 54?[2]

Playing these sorts of games will make mental mathematics become second nature – it will also give you lots of activities to enjoy with the classes you teach.

Finally, as you try out the example questions in the book, set yourself questions that follow the same format. Even better, set questions for your friends, ask them to answer them and then mark them and, if they get them wrong, show them where they have made mistakes. Posing questions and then solving them is a great way to learn mathematics. This is another technique you can use with your pupils.

Literacy

Read

The best way to become more literate is to read more. But try to notice what you are reading. Analyse the punctuation; ask yourself why the writer has chosen to use punctuation in that way. Make lists of any words that you don't know – use the 'look, cover, write, check' method to learn to spell them. Find out the meanings from a dictionary. Try to work out how you say the words; use the internet to find out the correct pronunciation. Read a range of different genres – if you mainly read novels, begin to read non-fiction. Start to read the educational press so that you get used to reading the literature that you will need to draw on in the test and in your course in the future.

Analyse the reports that you read – list the key facts from each section as you read it.

Act as a sub editor

As you read your daily paper or the educational reports, split the text up and add subheadings. Check spellings and punctuation – there are often errors, particularly in newspapers because they are often put together very quickly. Select sentences at random and try to rewrite them so that they read better. You could also write a three-sentence summary of the key points of the article.

Spelling tests

Give a friend your list of new words, or words that you often misspell. Get them to test you. Or alternatively you test them and explain to them how you remember the spelling patterns. If you are using teaching resources produced by yourself, make some deliberate mistakes in your spelling (but not too many!) and get the pupils to identify them. This might also get you off the hook if you make some unintentional errors!

Notice grammatical errors

Whenever you see an apostrophe on a sign or in the newspaper, ask yourself if it is correct. You will come to realise that many people use apostrophes incorrectly! Do the same with colons and semicolons – of course, you need to read Chapter 8 first, so that you can make sure you are correct.

If you can use this period of study as a reason to enjoy learning mathematics and literacy, you will be a much better teacher when you share your passion with the learners in your care. Try to get into the habit of seeing mathematics and literacy all around you. This will not only help you 'revise' for the tests, but will also help you begin to see what you can talk about on a day-to-day basis with the pupils you teach.

Now it is time to get stuck into the subject knowledge. Look back at the audit test you have carried out. Prioritise the areas you need to work on and let's get started.

Notes

1   England won 58 gold medals, the population of England is 53.5 million, so as a percentage the gold medals won works out as $58/53,500,000 \times 100 = 0.0001\%$. Scotland won 19 gold medals, the population of Scotland is 5,313,600, so as a percentage this works out as $19/5,313,600 \times 100 = 0.0003\%$. So, by my calculations Scotland did three times as well as England!
2   I managed $121 \div 2 = 60.5$ as the closest, or $21 \times 2 + 1 = 43$. Can you do any better? Try it with the time as you read this footnote and your own age!

4 Mastering the mental arithmetic test

This chapter explains:

- The format of the questions that you will be asked in the mental arithmetic test.
- All the subjects you need to answer these questions correctly.

In this chapter I cover all the areas of mathematics that you will be asked about in the mental test. It is important that you initially focus on the content rather than try to answer the questions quickly. Speed will come, but become confident with the mathematics first. Students have often come to me frustrated and nervous because they have taken a practice test and only got one or two correct. 'It isn't fair', they say, 'I know that I could do the questions but I didn't have enough time to think about the answers'. My advice would be to try out a practice test first to see where you are at that moment in time. You might be able to get most of the answers correct – in this case just use the book to remind yourself of the areas that are still causing you problems. It would not be unusual to only get one or two correct. If this describes you then work your way carefully through the chapter.

In each section I have given you the question and the answer. Giving the answer is deliberate. This allows you to focus on the strategies you are using to find the answer rather than worrying too much about the answer being correct. Of course the correct answer is vital, but when you are preparing it is more important that you understand the strategies you are using. This means you can use these strategies successfully for a whole range of questions.

In a notebook, write down the question and the answer and then write down how you worked out the answer – give as much detail as you can. If you can think of more than one way to work out the answer, that is great. You can then compare this with the range of strategies given in the text. The more strategies that you have to answer the mental arithmetic questions, the better your chance of getting the question correct in the given time.

Once you have worked through the chapter, try a practice test from the Department of Education website (http://sta.education. gov.uk).

Give yourself extra time by selecting that option. If you still can't answer within the time, don't panic; simply go through the questions and answer as many as you can. Then go back through the test writing down the questions and work them out in your own time. This allows you to sort out the questions that you can do given enough time and those that you still don't understand. Revisit those areas to remind yourself of the mathematics and then try the test again.

You will gradually be able to answer the questions in shorter amounts of time the more times you repeat the process.

Each section contains a range of questions for you to try out. If you find you are answering these confidently, or find them easy, then jump to the next section. The sections are:

1   *Time*: You might be asked a question about organising timed interviews at a parents' evening.

2   *Money*: You may be asked to convert between currencies in the context of a school trip or about the costs of buying resources.

3 *Fractions, decimals and percentages*: You will be asked questions that involve adding, subtracting, multiplying and dividing using fractions, decimals and percentages.

4 *Proportions*: This may be about proportions in terms of boys and girls in your class. Questions are often linked to assessment results or percentage increase and decrease if you are making purchasing decisions.

5 *Measurements*: These questions could be linked to distance and time or about lengths, areas or volumes. As with other questions in the test, the context that will be used will be everyday mathematics that you may have to deal with in the classroom.

Time

Remember:

- Using the 24-hour clock is easy – if the time is in the afternoon, just add 12 to the hour. So 1 pm = 13:00 and 4 pm = 16:00 and so on.

- Work with hours and minutes separately – it doesn't matter which you start with. The same applies to years and months.

- Don't forget there are 60 minutes in an hour and 12 months in a year. If your answer has more than 60 minutes or 12 months in it, it is wrong.

Question 1

A pupil who is new to your class has an actual age of 11 years and 8 months. An assessment report states that her reading age is 13 months above her actual age. What is the pupil's reading age in years and months?

Answer: 12 years 9 months

Calculation strategy

First you need to make sure you are carrying out the correct operation. Her reading age is 'above' her actual age so her reading age will be greater than her actual age. This means you add 13 months to 11 years 8 months.

13 months is the same as 1 year and 1 month and then

11 years 8 months + 13 months
= 11 years 8 months + 1 year 1 month
= 12 years 9 months

Question 2

The first lesson in the afternoon starts at 12:45. You have planned an introductory activity that will take 15 minutes, then an individual activity that will last 25 minutes, followed by 10 minutes for group discussion before you start a plenary. What time will the plenary start? Give you answer using the 24-hour clock.

Answer: 13:35

Calculation strategies

Calculate the total length of the activities by adding together 15 + 25 + 10 = 50 minutes.

50 minutes is 10 minutes less than 1 hour.

12:45 + 1 hour = 13:45,

so subtract 10 minutes from this to give 13:35.

Alternatively you could add the separate activities on to the start time, keeping a cumulative answer (running total).

12:45 + 15 minutes = 13:00

13:00 + 25 minutes = 13:25

13:25 + 10 minutes = 13:35

If you find these sorts of calculations difficult, try to visualise a clock face and move the hands to help you.

Question 3

A parents' evening begins at 17:30. You are seeing 15 parents and each appointment is 10 minutes long. When will you finish your last appointment? Give your answer using the 24-hour clock.

Answer: 20:00

Calculation strategies
You first need to calculate the total time taken up by appointments. This is:

15 × 10 minutes = 150 minutes = 2 hours 30 minutes

(15 × 10 is straightforward. I know there are 60 minutes in an hour, so there are 120 minutes in two hours. 120 + 30 = 150, so 150 minutes = 2 hours 30 minutes.)

Now add 2 hours 30 minutes to 17:30.

17:30 + 2 hours = 19:30

19:30 + 30 minutes = 20:00

Or

17:30 + 30 minutes = 18:00

18:00 + 2 hours = 20:00

(Luckily, whichever way you do it, you get the same answer – mathematics is good like that!)

Question 4

The afternoon session at school starts at 13:00. There are three lessons of 45 minutes and one break of 15 minutes. What time does the afternoon session finish?

Answer: 15:30

Calculation strategies

As with previous questions, you can either keep a cumulative total:

13:00 + 45 minutes = 13:45

13:45 + 45 minutes = 14:30 (This is where visualising a clock face helps – there are 15 minutes from 13:45, or a quarter to 2, to 2 o'clock. This leaves us with 30 minutes, which takes us to 14:30 or half past 2.)

14:30 + 45 minutes = 15:15

15:15 + 15 minutes = 15:30

Or

Three lessons of 45 minutes gives 135 minutes or 2 hours 15 minutes. You may have added 45 + 45 to give 90 minutes and realised this is 1 hour 30 minutes (1½ hours). You can then add another 45 minutes to give 2 hours 15 minutes.

Adding the break of 15 minutes gives a total of 2 hours 30 minutes.

13:00 + 2 hours 30 minutes = 15:30

Money

Remember:

- Money is easier than time because everything works in units of 100. There are 100 pence in a pound.

- Partitioning is a useful method to simplify mental multiplication calculations.

Question 1

You recommend that pupils on a language exchange trip take £50 spending money with them. If 1.6 Euros equal £1, how many Euros is this?

Answer: 80 Euros

Calculation strategies

1.6 Euro = £1, so for every pound you will receive 1.6 Euros. This means the calculation is:

1.6 × 50 (as we have £50)

1.6 is between 1 and 2, so the answer is between 50 and 100. It is always worth estimating the answer first.

One method is to multiply 16 × 50 and then divide by 10. So:

16 × 50 = 10 × 50 + 6 × 50 = 500 + 300 = 800

Meaning 1.6 × 50 = 80.

Alternatively 1.6 × 50 = 1 × 50 + 0.6 × 50
$$= 50 + 30$$
$$= 80$$

Both of these methods use *partitioning*. This means splitting a big number up into smaller numbers to make calculating easier.

Question 2

You run a book club savings scheme. Pupils save 25 p per school week over the year to spend at a book fair. It is 27 school weeks until the book fair. How much will they have to spend?

Answer: £6.75

Calculation strategies

Saving 25 p per week means you save you save £1 every 4 weeks.

27 weeks is one week less than 28 weeks.

I would have saved £7 in 28 weeks, so I save £6.75.

Alternatively the calculation is 0.25 × 27.

This is the same as 25 × 27 if I divide my answer by 100.

$$25 \times 27 = 20 \times 27 + 5 \times 27$$
$$= 540 + 135 \ (5 \times 20 = 100, \ 5 \times 7 = 35)$$
$$= 675, \text{ giving } £6.75.$$

This is a good example of checking that the answer you get is sensible. If you can't remember where the decimal place should go, then you can check by estimating. It would clearly be unrealistic for pupils to have either £67.50 or £675 if they are only saving 25 p a week.

Question 3

You need to buy pencils for the department. You buy 10 boxes of 12 pencils for £60.00. What is the cost per pencil?

Answer: 50 p

Calculation strategy

10 boxes cost £60.00, so 1 box costs £6.00.

To calculate the cost of 1 pencil we need to calculate:

£6.00 ÷ 12 = 50 p

You may notice that 2 pencils cost £1 because 12 pencils cost £6. If 2 pencils cost £1, then 1 pencil costs 50 p.

Question 4

You attend a planning meeting with the local university. They pay travel costs at 40 p per mile. Your journey is 9.5 miles each way. How much can you claim?

Answer: £7.60

Calculation strategy

The first thing to notice is that you are only given the mileage for one way. It is a return journey, so you have to calculate the round trip. The journey is 9.5 miles each way, so you travel a total of 19 miles.

The calculation is now:

$$19 \times 40 = 10 \times 40 + 9 \times 40$$
$$= 400 + 360$$
$$= 760 \text{ p}$$
$$= £7.60$$

You may find it easier to calculate $20 \times 40 = 800$ then subtract 20 to give 760.

Alternatively you could calculate the amount you claim for one way.

$$9.5 \times 40 \text{ p} = 9 \times 40 \text{ p} + 0.5 \times 40 \text{ p}$$
$$= 3.60 + 0.20$$
$$= £3.80$$

If I can claim £3.80 for one way, I double this for the total claim, giving £7.60.

Fractions, decimals and percentages

Remember:

- Percentages are always out of 100. To change a percentage to a fraction write it down as a fraction out of 100 and then cancel the fraction down to its simplest form.

- You can find 10% of any number by dividing by 10. This is because 10% is equivalent to 1/10.

A fraction is made up of a numerator and a denominator.

4 (The numerator – the number of parts of the whole)

___

7 (The denominator – the number of parts the whole has been divided into)

Or as a picture:

Fractions can be simplified by finding a number that will divide into the numerator and the denominator. These are called equivalent fractions. For example:

1/2 = 2/4 = 4/8 = 8/16 = 16/32

1/4 = 2/8 = 3/12 = 4/16

And so on.

If you divide by a fraction or a decimal less than 1, you get a larger answer. So:

156 ÷ 0.1 = 1560

156 ÷ 0.01 = 15,600

and so on.

You can make addition and subtraction easier by partitioning. So:

27 × 8 = 20 × 8 + 7 × 8
       = 160 + 56
       = 216

65 + 37 = (60 + 30) + (5 + 7)
        = 90 + 12
        = 102

Question 1

In a Year 9 assessment, 80% of the marks come from a written paper and 20% from coursework. 1/4 of the marks in the written paper come from a mental test. What fraction of the total marks come from the mental test?

Answer: 1/5

Calculation strategies

Make sure you read the question carefully and don't just jump to an answer. Students have sometimes answered 25% because they have just worked out 1/4 as a decimal without realising that we actually need to work out 1/4 of 80%.

Mastering the mental arithmetic test

80% of the marks come from the written paper.

1/4 of 80% = 20% (80 ÷ 4 = 20)

20% = 20/100

20/100 = 1/5 (cancel by dividing numerator and denominator by 20)

Question 2

There are 125 pupils in Year 6. 80% achieved a level 4 or level 5 in the Key Stage 2 mathematics. 35 pupils achieved a level 5. How many pupils achieved level 4?

Answer: 65

Calculation strategies

80% achieved level 4 or 5

80% of 125 = 100 pupils

(You may know that 10% = 12.5 and 8 × 12.5 = 100 or you may notice that 80% is the same as 4/5. 1/5 of 125 is 25, dividing 125 by 5. So 4/5 is 100 as 4 × 25 = 100.)

So 100 pupils achieved level 4 or 5.

If 35 achieved a grade 5, then 100 − 35 = 65 pupils achieved level 4.

Question 3

There are 150 pupils in Year 11. 30 pupils achieved an A or A* in English. What percentage of pupils achieved an A or A* in English?

Answer: 20%

Calculation strategies

30/150 pupils achieved A or A*.

We need to change this to a fraction with 100 as the denominator to work out the percentage.

Dividing by 3 gives 30/150 = 10/50.

Doubling the numerator and the denominator
10/50 = 20/100 = 20%.

Alternatively 30/150 = 1/5 (dividing numerator and
denominator by 30)

1/5 = 20% (as 5 × 20 = 100)

Question 4

Your pupils are carrying out an experiment. They suggest that a car will travel 40% further if they increase the slope of a ramp. Before they increase the slope the car travels 60 cm. How far will it travel this time? Give the answer in cm.

Answer: 84 cm

Calculation strategies

We need to calculate 40% of 60 cm.

10% of 60 = 6 cm (we can find 10% of any number by
dividing by 10)

So 40% = 24 cm (40% is 10 times as much as 10%)

It travels 40% further, so we need to add:

60 + 24 = 84 cm

Question 5

You have 25 pupils in your class. 12 of them get full marks in a mental mathematics test. What percentage of your class got full marks?

Answer: 48%

Calculation strategies

As a fraction, 12/25 pupils got full marks.

Multiplying the numerator and denominator by 4:

12/25 = 48/100 = 48%

This looks right because just less than half your class got full marks. It is always worth checking an answer in this way.

Question 6

You have a class of 30 pupils. 25 have English as an Additional Language (EAL). What fraction of your class have EAL? Give your answer as a fraction in its simplest form.

Answer: 5/6

Calculation strategies
As a fraction, 25/30 have EAL

25 and 30 will both divide by 5 so

25/30 is the same as 5/6

Question 7

The activities on a cross-curricula day are budgeted at £60. Travel should cost 15% of the total. What is the amount you can spend on travel?

Answer: £9

Calculation strategies
Start by thinking about facts that you know. You can probably remember that you find 10% by dividing by 10, so:

10% of £60 = £6 (dividing by 10)

5% of £60 = £3 (5% is half of 10%)

15% = 6 + 3 = £9

Question 8

What is 592 ÷ 0.1?

Answer: 5920

Calculation strategies

This is the type of question that most candidates get wrong. It may be that there is a common misconception that division always gives a smaller answer. This is not the case when dividing by fractions. If you think of the questions as 'How many tenths are there in 59?', you can see that there will be ten times as many as the number you start with 0.1 is the same as 1/10.

Similarly 4 ÷ 1/2 = 8 (there are 8 halves in 4)

or 3 ÷ 1/5 = 15 (there are 15 fifths in 3)

Question 9

In your year group there are 3 classes of 26 pupils and 2 classes of 29 pupils. What is the total number of pupils in the year group?

Answer: 136

Calculation strategies

3 × 26 = 78 (3 × 20 = 60 and 3 × 6 = 18 and 60 + 18 = 78)

2 × 29 = 58 (2 × 20 = 40 and 2 × 9 = 18 and 40 + 18 = 58, or
2 × 30 = 60 and 60 − 2 = 58)

78 + 58 = 136 (70 + 50 = 120 and 8 + 8 = 16 and
120 + 16 = 136)

Question 10

The school's policy is to employ one teaching assistant for every 15 pupils. There are 169 pupils in the year group. How many teaching assistants should the school employ?

Answer: 12

Calculation strategies

You know that 10 × 15 = 150, so 11 × 15 = 165.

So 165 ÷ 15 = 11 remainder 4.

There are 169 pupils, so you will need an extra teaching assistant to make sure there is one for every 15 pupils, giving 12 teaching assistants.

Proportions

Remember:

- Ratio compares part with part. If you have a class of 25 with 10 boys and 15 girls, then the ratio of boys to girls is 10 to 15. We would write 10:15. Because both 10 and 15 divide by 5, we can 'cancel' this down to make the ratio 2:3. Another way of saying this is that there are 3 girls for every 2 boys. It is perhaps easier to see this diagrammatically:

B	B	G	G	G
B	B	G	G	G
B	B	G	G	G
B	B	G	G	G
B	B	G	G	G

You can see there are 25 pupils arranged in groups of 5. In each group there are 2 boys and 3 girls.

- Proportion is different from the ratio in that it compares a part with the whole. So the proportion of the class who are boys is 10 out of the whole class – that is 10 out of 25. We can write this as a fraction:

10/25, which we can cancel down to 2/5, meaning 2/5 of the class are boys.

We could write this as a decimal: 2/5 is the same as 0.4. I work this out by dividing 2 by 5 and $2 \div 5 = 0.4$.

I could also write it down as a percentage:

0.4 is the same as 40% ($0.4 \times 100 = 40$)

Question 1

In the year group at a primary school there are 120 pupils. 72 pupils are boys. What proportion of the year group are girls? Give your answer as a decimal.

Answer: 0.4

Calculation strategy
There are 120 pupils in total. 72 of them are boys so 48 are girls (120 − 72 = 48).

As a fraction, 48/120 are girls, which can be cancelled down to 4/10 by dividing the numerator (the top number) and the denominator (the bottom number) by 12.

In the mental arithmetic questions you will always be able to cancel the fractions down to a number you can change to a decimal because you cannot use a calculator in the actual test.

4/10 = 0.4 as a decimal

Question 2

There are 60 pupils in Year 6. 15 pupils achieved level 5 in mathematics. What proportion of pupils achieved level 5 in mathematics? Give your answer as a decimal.

Answer: 0.25

Calculation strategy
The answer is 15/60 as a fraction because there are 15 boys out of a class of 60.

This can be cancelled down to 1/4. You may also spot that there are four fifteens in 60, which means that the fraction is the same as a quarter.

1/4 = 0.25 as a decimal

Try to remember common fractions as decimals and percentages. For example:

1/4 = 0.25 = 25% (because 1/4 of 100 is 25)

1/2 = 0.5 = 50% (because 1/2 of 100 is 50)

3/4 = 0.75 = 75% (because 3/4 of 100 is 75)

Measurements

Remember:

* There are 1000 ml in 1 litre; 1000 g in a kilogram, 100 cm in a metre.

Question 1

You are looking at an atlas and find that the distance between two towns in Germany is 96 km. As an approximation, 8 km is equal to 5 miles. What is this distance in miles?

Answer: 60 miles

Calculation strategies
Every 8 km is 5 miles approximately.

The distance between the two towns is 96 km and

96 is 8 × 12 (8 × 10 = 80 and 2 × 8 = 16)

So multiply 12 × 5 to find how many miles = 60.

Question 2

You are making juice for your class. You give each pupil 150 ml of juice. There are 25 pupils in the class. How much juice do you need? Give your answer in litres.

Answer: 3.75 litres

Calculation strategies

First multiply 150 × 25.

I know 100 × 25 = 2500,

so 50 × 25 = 1250 (half as much)

150 × 25 = 2500 + 1250

= 3750 ml

There are 1000 ml in a litre so 3750 ml = 3.75 litres.

(Again this sounds 'about right'. You need four litre-boxes of juice for a class.)

Question 3

You are cooking with your class and each pupil needs 125 g of flour. You buy flour in 1.5-kg packs. There are 20 pupils cooking with you. How many bags of flour do you need to buy?

Answer: 2

Calculation strategies

You need 125 × 20 = 2500 g of flour.

2500 g = 2.5 kg

So you will need 2 bags (3 kg) to make sure you have enough flour.

I hope the mental test makes more sense to you now. You have an understanding of the sorts of questions that you might be asked and have worked through a range of strategies that you can use to help you with your mental arithmetic skills.

5 Success in the written questions

This chapter explains:

- All the facts and information you need to successfully tackle the questions in the 'on-screen' section of the test.
- The style of questions that you will be asked.
- The way you should practise to study the areas of 'number' that you feel you need to develop.

What do you already know?

Each section of this chapter opens with a review of the key mathematical concepts that you will need to answer the questions that follow. Read through this and then answer the questions in each section. Use your notebook to work out the answer before you look at the answer in the book. And use a calculator! An on-screen calculator is available for you when you take the test. The questions in the book are in the same format as the questions you will see in the written part of the skills test. When you have tried the questions, look at the answers. This will help you focus on the areas that you need to study. Focus on the areas that you are unsure of rather than trying to cover everything. If you feel comfortable with the question at the beginning of the section, skip over the rest of the content and try the question that opens the next section.

In this chapter I would like you to work out the question for yourself in your notebook before you look at the strategy I would use and the answer. The areas that are covered in the written section of the test are:

- time
- money
- proportion and ratio
- percentages, fractions and decimals, including converting fractions to decimals and percentages
- measurements (for example, finding a distance or an area)
- conversions (for example, converting from one currency to another)
- averages (including mean, median, mode and range), interpreting charts and graphs
- using simple formulae.

You will also see a range of ways of representing data. These are usually straightforward, but you may find diagrams or charts that you are not familiar with. Don't panic – the examples will show you how to interpret these diagrams and charts.

Time

Questions testing you on your understanding of time are usually of three types.

- Reading timetables correctly.
- Planning activities such as a parents' evening or different sections of a lesson.
- Planning for travel – this often includes conversions (see conversions section below).

Success in the written questions

For all of these questions you will need to know:

- **The 24-hour clock:** To convert a time in the afternoon to the 24-hour clock you simply add 12. This is because the afternoon starts at 12:00. So:

    2 pm = 14:00

    5 pm = 17:00

    9:45 pm = 21:45

    And so on.

- **Adding units of time:** First of all remember that there are 60 minutes in an hour. Then you can add the minutes together until you get to 60 minutes, which means you have made a full hour. (See question 1 below.)

Question 1

You have parents' consultations over two evenings that start at 17:30. You can book appointments that last 10 minutes. You are expected to take a 20-minute break each evening. There are 24 parents who have booked appointments. You fill all the slots on the first evening and finish at 20:00.

If you fill all the available slots and take a break, what time will you finish on the second evening? Give your answer using the 24-hour clock.

Calculation strategies

Look at the first evening.

You start at 17:30 and finish at 20:00.

This is 2.5 hours or 150 minutes because
2 × 60 = 120 and 120 + 30 = 150 (30 minutes = half an hour)

150 − 20 = 130 (I have taken off the 20-minute break)

130 ÷ 10 = 13 (each appointment is 10 minutes)

So on the first evening I have seen 13 parents. There are 24 to see altogether, so I will need to see 11 parents on the second evening (24 − 13 = 11).

11 parents at 10 minutes each = 11 × 10 = 110 minutes

110 + 20 = 130 (adding the 20-minute break)

130 minutes = 2 hours 10 minutes (1 hour is 60 minutes)

So I need to know the time 2 hours and 10 minutes after 17:30.

Answer: 19:40

Question 2

You are driving the school minibus to a youth hostel. The youth hostel is 275 km from school. You know that you will drive at an average speed of 50 km per hour, but you have to take a break of 20 minutes every 2 hours. You must arrive at the youth hostel at 17:00. What time should you leave school?

Calculation strategies

This looks very complicated, but let's break the question down. After all, planning efficiently for a trip with your class helps everyone enjoy it.

You travel at an average of 50 km per hour. That means in 2 hours you will cover 100 km.

In a table:

Activity	Time taken
Drive 100 km	2 hours
Break	20 minutes
Drive 100 km	2 hours
Break	20 minutes
Drive 75 km	1½ hours = 1 hour 30 minutes

Success in the written questions

Activity	Time taken
Arrive	
Total time	5 hours 40 minutes + 30 minutes = 6 hours 10 minutes

This table shows that you break for 20 minutes every 2 hours. So, after 2 hours, when you have travelled 100 km, you break for 20 minutes. Then you can set off again – travel for another 2 hours, covering another 100 km before taking another break. You have now covered 200 km, which means there are 75 km to go. You know that you cover 50 km in an hour, so you can see it takes half an hour to cover 25 km (25 is half of 50), so it takes 1½ hours to cover 75 km.

To find the total time I added up the hours (2 + 2 + 1), which gave me 5 hours.

Then I added up the minutes. 20 + 20 + 30 = 70 minutes = 1 hour 10 minutes.

5 hours + 1 hour 10 minutes = 6 hours 10 minutes

We haven't quite finished.

We know:

* The journey takes 6 hours 10 minutes.
* We have to get there by 17:00 (5 o'clock in the afternoon).

This means we have to leave 1 hour and 10 minutes before noon because it is 5 hours from noon to 5 pm and 6 hours 10 minutes – 5 hours leaves 1 hour 10 minutes.

So we need to leave at 10:50. You don't need to write am because we are using the 24-hour clock.

Answer: 10.50

Money

Calculations using money usually relate to purchasing materials for school. You can see that being able to calculate using money is a useful skill for a teacher to have. The good thing about calculating with money is that you just have to remember how to work with decimals. These questions sometimes involve working with percentages too.

Question 1

You are going to buy packs of pens for your department. You need 25 packs. You are researching to find out if it is cheaper to buy from a catalogue or from the internet. Complete the table by choosing the correct answer from the choices below.

Seller	Cost per pack	Offers	Postage	Total
Catalogue	£5.50	Buy 10 packs get one free	£1.50 per pack	?
Internet	£5.80	Free postage	No postage charge	?

| £126.50 | £135.00 | £164.00 | £145.00 |

Calculation strategies

Catalogue:

Packs cost £5.50 per pack

10 packs cost £55.00

20 packs cost £110.00 (multiply 55 × 2)

Success in the written questions

We get 2 packs free, so we need a further 3 packs.

$3 \times £5.50 = £16.50$ $(3 \times £5 = £15;$
$3 \times 50 \text{ p} = £1.50;$
$£5 + £1.50 = £6.50)$

Adding together:

$£110.00 + £16.50 = £126.50$

This is the cost for the pens. Now we need to add on the postage:

$£25 \times £1.50$ (partition the £1.50 into £1 + 50 p)

$25 \times £1 = £25$

$25 \times 50 \text{ p} = £12.50$ (this is also a half of 25, because 50 p is half of £1)

Total postage = £37.50

So the total cost is $£126.50 + £37.50 = £164.00$
($50 \text{ p} + 50 \text{ p} = £1$ and $£126 + £37 = £163$, then add the extra £1)

Answer = £164.00

Notice that one of the answers offered was to add £126.50, which is the total without postage. Don't assume that you have the correct answer simply because it is one of the choices available. The 'wrong' answers may be decoys.

Internet: There is no postage, so we simply need to work out:

$£5.80 \times 25$. As above

$10 \times £5.80 = £58.00$

$10 \times £5.80 = £58.00$

$5 \times £5.80 = £29.00$ (divide 58 by 2)

Answer: £145

Question 2

You are going to take your class to the zoo at the end of term. There will be 30 people on the trip, including adults and children. The tickets cost £60 for each group of 10 people and the coach will cost £4.50 per person. How much does the trip cost per person?

Calculation strategies
The first thing to spot is that you need to work out the cost of entrance to the zoo per person and then add that to the coach cost, which is already given per person.

Total cost of zoo = £60 × 3 = £180.

There are 30 on the trip, so this is £6 each.

Alternatively just divide £60 by 10, giving £6 too.

The coach is £4.50 per person.

Total cost = £6.00 + £4.50 = £10.50.

Answer = £10.50

Question 3

You are an art teacher and are buying a range of materials for your class. You teach 125 students. You need to buy card, paint and brushes. The prices are:

Card: 5 p per sheet (you need 1000 sheets)

Paint: £3.50 per pack (enough for 25 pupils)

Brushes: £1.30 per pack (you need 3 packs for every 25 pupils)

How much will you need to spend?

Calculation strategies
Work it out item by item.

Success in the written questions

Card: $1000 \times 5 \text{ p} = 5000 \text{ p}$
$= £50.00$
(because $100 \text{ p} = £1$)

Paint: You need 5 packs $(125 \div 25 = 5)$

so $5 \times £3.50 = £17.50$

Brushes: You need 15 packs (3 packs for every 25 pupils: there are 125 pupils)

$£1.30 \times 15 = £19.50$

$(10 \times £1.30 = £13.00$ so $5 \times £1.30 = £6.50)$

Adding these together
$£50.00 + £17.50 + £19.50 = £87.00$

Answer $= £87.00$

Proportion and ratio

Working with proportions and ratios relies on you having a good understanding of fractions.

Remember

Ratio compares part to part. 1 to every 4 is a ratio. For example, there is one adult to every four children on a school trip. The ratio of adults to children is 1:4. The ratio of children to adults is 4:1.

Proportion compares part to the whole. 1 out of 5 is a proportion. 1 out of every 5 people on the trip is an adult. 4 out of 5 people on the trip are children.

1/5 is a fraction. 1/5 of the people on the trip are adults. 4/5 of the people on the trip are children. Proportions are often expressed as a percentage. If 1/5 of the people are adults we need to work out 1/5 as a percentage. This is 20% because 1/5 of 100 is 20. I find this by dividing 100 by 5.

Question 1

Your school is organising a sponsored silence to raise money for charity. You agree to divide the money between the charity and the school funds in the ratio 3:1. This table shows how much money each class raised.

Class	Amount raised
Class 1	£24.00
Class 2	£32.50
Class 3	£30.00
Class 4	£35.00
Class 5	£38.00
Class 6	£42.50

How much money is given to the charity?

Calculation strategies

First add up the total = £202.00.

We are dividing in the ratio 3:1, so we split it into four 'shares'.

The school gets one 'share' and the charity gets three 'shares'.

£202 ÷ 4 = £50.50 (200 ÷ 4 = 50 and 2 ÷ 4 = 0.5)

So each share = £50.50

The charity gets 3 shares, so 3 × £50.50 = £151.50.

Answer: £151.50

Question 2

Look at the table below, which shows the maths sets in which the 15 pupils with English as Additional Language in your tutor group have been placed. What proportion are in set 1? Give your answer as a percentage.

Pupil	Set
A	Set 2
B	Set 3
C	Set 1
D	Set 4
E	Set 2
F	Set 1
G	Set 1
H	Set 3
I	Set 2
J	Set 1
K	Set 4
L	Set 1
M	Set 5
N	Set 2
O	Set 1

Calculation strategies

There are 6 pupils in the top set. There are 15 pupils altogether, so 6 out of 15 are in the top set.

6/15 is a fraction. We can divide the top and bottom by 3 to cancel the fraction down:

6/15 = 2/5

We need to change this to a percentage. Percentages are out of 100. 100 ÷ 5 is 20. This means 1/5 is the same as 20%.

If 1/5 is 20%, then 2/5 (twice as big as 1/5) is 40%

So 6/15 = 2/5 = 40%

Answer: 40%

Percentages, fractions and decimals

Before you read on, write 1/2 in the centre of a fresh page in your notebook. Create a web diagram that shows all the different ways you can write or represent 1/2. These could be *equivalent fractions* (so 4/8 is the same as 1/2 – we say 4/8 is an equivalent fraction to 1/2); you may know that 50% is the same as 1/2, and so on.

The point of this activity is to show you how closely related fractions, decimals and percentages are. In fact they are all just different ways of writing down 'parts of a whole'. Just another way of saying 2 and a bit. We need to know exactly what 'the bit' is if we are going to carry out calculations.

Fractions

There is specific language associated with fractions that you may have forgotten.

$\dfrac{5}{7}$ (Numerator – or the number of parts we need)

(Denominator – or the number of parts the whole is divided into)

So this fraction is five-sevenths – we have divided something into 7 parts and are interested in 5 of these 7 parts.

Simplifying fractions may be something that you have forgotten how to do. This is sometimes called *cancelling down*. There are some fractions that you 'just know' are the same. In the opening activity you may have written a whole list of equivalent fractions such as 1/2 = 2/4 = 4/8 = 8/16 or 3/6 = 6/12 and so on.

All you need to remember is that to simplify a fraction you need to find a number that will divide exactly into the numerator and the denominator. So:

$$\frac{15}{20} = \frac{3}{4}$$

both 15 and 20 will divide by 5

15 (15 ÷ 5 = 3) = 3

20 (20 ÷ 5 = 4) = 4

Percentages

Percentages are always 'out of 100'. You could see these as a special sort of fraction. One where the denomination is always 100. You will know the % sign from the media and from examination results. I remember a pupil once saying to me 'I got 58%, but I don't know how many it was out of.' The % sign means that whatever the test was out of it has been converted, so it is 'out of 100'.

So, for example, if I get 18 out of 25 in a test that is the same as 72%. Why?

$$\frac{18}{25}$$ as a fraction 'is equivalent to' (the same as) $$\frac{72}{100}$$

I know that 4 × 25 = 100, so I multiply 18 × 4 to keep the fraction the same.

$$\frac{72}{100}$$ is a percentage, so I can write 72%.

Decimals

Decimals are another way to describe parts of a whole. When we use decimals we always work with tenths, hundredths, thousandths and so on. We separate the whole numbers from the decimal fractions by a decimal point.

So 5.6592 means:

5 units	decimal point	6 tenths	5 hundredths	9 thousandths	2 ten thousandths
5	.	6	5	9	2

As before, the best way to make more sense of these ideas is to try out the examples.

Question 1

At a staff meeting the mathematics coordinator gives out the following table to show the number of pupils in each class who have been identified as needing intervention support in mathematics.

What percentage of pupils in the school require intervention support? Give your answer to the nearest whole number.

Class	Number of pupils in class	Number of pupils needing intervention support
Year 1	28	4
Year 2	32	3
Year 3	31	5
Year 4	29	3
Year 5	27	3
Year 6	26	6

Calculation strategies

First we need to work out the number of pupils needing intervention as a fraction of the total number of pupils:

Total number of pupils = 28 + 32 + 31 + 29 + 27 + 26
= 173

(Always add the numbers up twice – I add them up in a different order each time to check I have the correct answer.)

Number of pupils needing support = 4 + 3 + 5 + 3 + 3 + 6
= 24

So, as a fraction this is 24/173. We can change this to a decimal by dividing 24 by 173. Using the calculator, this is the same as:

24/173 = 0.138728

To convert this to a percentage we multiply by 100 (a percentage is always 'out of' 100).

0.138728 × 100 = 13.8728 . . .

To the nearest whole number, this is 14% (we always round up if the first decimal place is 5 or more).

Answer = 14%

Question 2

You are comparing the marks of pupils in a weekly spelling test. You want to know who has improved by at least 10%. Which pupils in the list have improved by at least 10%?

Pupil	Test 1 (Mark out of 30)	Test 2 (Mark out of 30)
A	22	24
B	20	24
C	18	21

Pupil	Test 1 (Mark out of 30)	Test 2 (Mark out of 30)
D	21	21
E	14	18
F	23	22
G	17	19
H	18	22

Calculation strategies

To find out what a 10% increase would be we need to know 10% of the score the pupils got in the first test. To find 10% of something, we divide by 10 (because 100 ÷ 10 = 10).

So, for example, 10% of 22 = 2.2 and 10% of 20 = 2.

The table below shows who improved by at least 10%. The complication is that the percentages are often decimals, while the test is marked out of 'whole numbers'. So pupils A got 22 in test 1. 10% of 22 is 2.2, so they need to get at least 24.2 in the next test (22 + 2.2 = 24.2). This is impossible, so they need to get 25 because this is the next whole number above 24.2.

Pupil	Result in test 1	10% of mark	Result in test 2	Improved by at least 10% of mark?
A	22	2.3	24	No
B	20	2.0	24	Yes
C	18	1.8	21	Yes
D	21	2.1	21	No
E	14	1.4	18	Yes
F	23	2.3	22	No

Success in the written questions

Pupil	Result in test 1	10% of mark	Result in test 2	Improved by at least 10% of mark?
G	17	1.7	19	Yes
H	18	1.8	22	No

Answer: Pupils B, C, E and G

Question 3

Your headteacher provides you with the following information in the form of a pie chart:

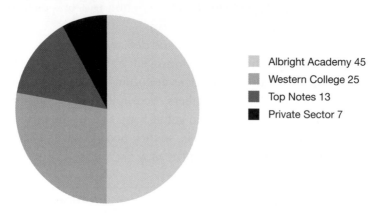

Albright Academy 45
Western College 25
Top Notes 13
Private Sector 7

Which of these statements are true?

A. More than 75% of pupils remained in the state sector.

B. More than 1/5 of the pupils went to Western College.

C. Less than 1 in 9 pupils moved to Top Notes Music Specialist College.

Answers:

There are a total of 90 pupils

75% of 90 is the same as 3/4 of 90

1/4 of 90 = 90 ÷ 4 = 22.5 so 3/4 = 67.5 (3 × 22.5)

83 pupils remained in the state sector (90 – 7)

Statement A is true

1/5 of 90 = 18 (90 ÷ 5 = 18)

25 pupils went to Western College

Statement B is true

1 in 9 pupils is the same as 10 pupils in 90 (multiplying both numbers by 10)

13 pupils moved to Top Notes

Statement C is true

Question 4

You gave your maths class a test at the beginning of a topic and another at the end of the topic. The bar chart below shows the two sets of results:

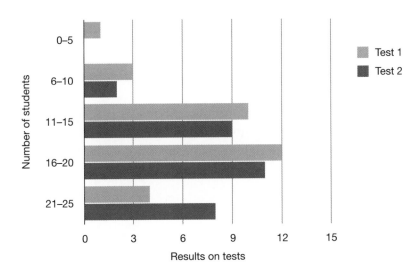

Success in the written questions

Which of these statements are true?

A. The number of pupils achieving 21 marks or higher increased by 75% from test 1 to test 2.

B. More than 50% of the pupils achieved 16 marks or higher in test 2.

C. The number of pupils achieving between 6 and 10 marks fell by 1/3.

Statement A is false: In test 1, 4 pupils achieved 21–25 marks and in test 2, 8 pupils. This is an increase of 4 pupils. This is 100% increase. This is the same as saying the number of pupils 'doubled'. (Note 100% of something is the same as 1 whole. So 100% of 32 pupils is 32 pupils, 100% of 16 boys is 16 boys and so on.)

Statement B is true: In test 2, 11 pupils achieved 16–20 marks and 8 pupils achieved 21–25. So a total of 19 pupils achieved 16 marks or higher. (Don't forget to add the two sets of pupils together.)

Adding together all the pupils who took test 2:

$0 + 2 + 9 + 11 + 8 = 30$

50% of 30 = 15 (50% is the same as 1/2)

19 pupils achieved 16 marks or higher. 19 is greater than 15.

Statement C is true: The number of pupils in this category fell from 3 to 2. That is, it fell by 1 pupil. As a fraction of the first value, this is 1/3 (1 out of 3 pupils moved out of this category for the second test). So the number of pupils fell by 1/3.

Measurements

These questions turn up less regularly than questions in the other sections. This isn't because they are hard, in fact they are usually very straightforward. You just need to remember:

- **Area** is the amount of space covered by something and is measured in square units.

- **Perimeter** is the distance around something. You can remember this if you think of phrases like 'Perimeter Fence'.

For example:

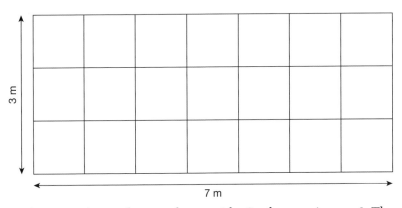

This room is 7 m long and 3 m wide. So the area is 21 m². The perimeter is 20 m. We can see there are 21 squares – all 1 m by 1 m. It is 20 m all the way round – 7 m along the top, then 3 m down, then another 7 m along the bottom and finally 3 m back up.

7 + 3 + 7 + 3 = 20

To find the area you multiply the length by the width. There is nothing magic about this formula. Think about any rectangle. To find the area you 'count the squares'. A quick way of counting the squares in the rectangle above is to notice that there are 3 rows of 7 squares. I can quickly 'count' by multiplying 3 × 7, or the length by the width.

Success in the written questions

Question 1

You give the school council responsibility for redecorating the school meeting room. It is 8 m long and 4.5 m wide. Carpet tiles are 1 m squares and cost £4.50 each. How much will it cost to carpet the room?

Calculation strategies

First find the area of the room.

We multiply the length by the width:

$8 \times 4.5 = 36$ m² $(8 \times 4 = 32$ and $8 \times 0.5 = 4)$

So I need 36 carpet tiles. To find out the cost:

$36 \times 4.50 = £162.00$ $(36 \times 4 = 144$ and
$36 \times 0.5 = 18$ as 0.5 is the same as
one half)

Answer: £162

Conversions

These questions focus on the types of conversions you may need to use in your job and indeed your everyday life. The two most common are currency conversion or miles to kilometres. You will always be given the conversion to use – for example, 5 miles is approximately 8 km.

Make sure you check your answers to see that you have used the correct operation for the conversion. For example, if you are converting miles to km your answer will be greater as 5 miles is 8 km. If you are converting from km to miles, your answer will be smaller and you will divide by 8 and multiply by 5.

As always, the best way to understand this is by trying out the questions.

Question 1

You are organising a school exchange to France. On the journey home you need to travel from Paris to Calais, a distance of 288 km. The coach driver tells you he estimates an average speed of 40 miles per hour from Paris to Calais. You need to be at the port for 19:30. What is the latest time you should leave Paris (use the estimate that 5 miles equals 8 km). Give your answer using the 24-hour clock.

Calculation strategies

First of all we need to convert 288 km to miles. 5 miles = 8 km so we need to divide by 8 and multiply by 5.

288 ÷ 8 = 36

36 × 5 = 180 miles (I actually used the on-screen calculator for both these calculations)

180 is less than 288 and we know that when we convert kilometres to miles we will get a smaller answer, so this looks about right.

The coach will travel at 40 miles per hour. This means we travel 40 miles for every hour of driving. So we need to work out how many 40s there are in 180.

180 ÷ 40 = 4.5. That means the journey will take 4½ hours.

This makes sense too as 40 + 40 + 40 + 40 + 20 = 180

We need to arrive at 19:30.

4½ hours before this is 15:00.

(4 hours before 7.30 pm is 3.30 pm and half an hour before this is 3 pm. In the 24-hour clock this is 15:00.)

Answer: The coach needs to leave at 15:00.

Success in the written questions

Question 2

You are planning a school trip to a youth hostel which is 275 miles away from school. It is an old minibus and the handbook states the fuel consumption is 28 miles per gallon. Fuel costs £1.35 per litre. How much will the fuel cost for the round trip. Use the conversion 1 gallon = 4.5 litres and give your answer to the nearest pound.

Calculation strategies

It is 275 miles to the youth hostel, so the round trip is:

$275 \times 2 = 550$ miles ($2 \times 200 = 400$ and $2 \times 75 = 150$)

Fuel consumption is 28 miles per gallon, so we need to work out how many gallons we will use:

$550 \div 28 = 19.643$ (I used the on-screen calculator and rounded to 3 decimal places)

This means we use 19.643 gallons, nearly 20 gallons. Again this sounds about right. Don't worry about the decimal places in the answer. The questions asked for an answer 'to the nearest'; this often means that you will get answers that need rounding up or down.

We are told that fuel costs £1.35 per litre, so I need to calculate:

$19.643 \times 1.35 = 26.5178$ (I round this up as the first decimal place is 5 or greater)

If you check to see that this is a sensible answer, it meets this criterion. A round trip like this would probably take about half a tank and £27 to half fill a minibus petrol tank seems 'about right'.

Answer: £27

Averages, including reading charts and graphs

Averages

There are three types of average that you will meet in the on-screen questions: mean, median and mode. The one that you will remember from school is the mean. However, the median and mode are just as useful as measures of a 'central' value of a set of numbers, or as a way of approximating a large set of data into a single number.

Mean

You probably use the 'mean' when you are thinking about where to go on holiday. You may consult charts that show you the 'mean' summer temperature of different places to see which is likely to be most conducive for a beach holiday (although these charts may simply use the word 'average', which is very unhelpful).

You calculate the mean by adding together all the numbers in the set and dividing by the number in the set. So to find the mean of:

14, 15, 16, 18, 18, 18, 21, 22

Add them all together and divide by 8

$$\frac{14 + 15 + 16 + 18 + 18 + 18 + 21 + 22}{8} = \frac{142}{8} = 17.75$$

Median

This is the middle number when the set is arranged in ascending order. It is often used when looking at the income of people. This is because a small number of people who earn huge sums of money will make the mean very high and so not reflect the earnings of most of the population.

Success in the written questions

To find the median of the set above, we arrange them in ascending order, so:

14, 15, 16, **18, 18**, 18, 21, 22

You can see that there are two numbers in the middle. Fortunately, they are both 18, so the median is 18.

If they had been different, for example:

14, 15, 16, **18, 19**, 20, 21, 22

We then take the number halfway between the two middle numbers. So the number halfway between 18 and 19 is 18.5.

For sets of data with an 'odd number' of entries it is easier, because there is only one middle number. For example, the median of:

15, 16, 18, **19**, 20, 21, 22

is 19.

Mode

The mode is the number that occurs most frequently or most often. If I was running a shoe shop, I would use the mode. This would make sure that I had plenty of shoes that would fit the majority of my customers.

So the mode of:

14, 15, 16, **18, 18, 18**, 21, 22

is 18.

Charts

There are several types of charts that you may see in the on-screen section. In fact, you have already worked with a comparison bar chart and a pie chart in the section on fractions, percentages and decimals. Have a look through the notes below and then try the questions. You will find that the best way to make sense of the charts is through trying the questions.

Bar charts

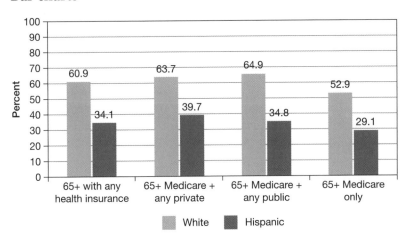

This is an example of a *comparison bar chart*. You read the information of the chart by finding the appropriate column or 'bar' and reading across to the axis with the scale on it. The two lines that contain the chart are called the 'axes'. The X axis runs horizontally and Y axis runs vertically.

Pie charts

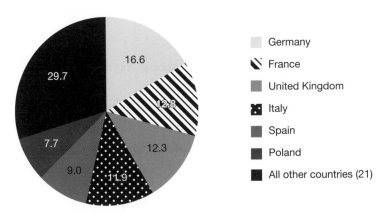

67

Success in the written questions

This is an example of a pie chart. Yes, it looks like a pie. Funny that. A pie chart is divided into sectors illustrating a numerical proportion. In a pie chart, the area of each 'slice' is proportional to the quantity it represents. Pie charts are very widely used, although it is difficult to compare different sections of a given pie chart, or to compare data across different pie charts. Bar charts are often a better way of illustrating data.

Scatter diagrams

A scatter diagram is drawn to compare two sets of data and to look for connections between the two sets of data. This is called correlation.

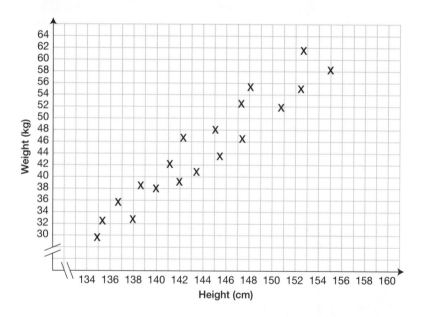

You have probably seen this type of diagram in the media. Each cross represents the height and weight of one person. You can see that the crosses slope up to the right. This shows that the taller you are, the heavier you are likely to be.

In the example above, the cross to the furthest point on the right shows the tallest person and the cross highest up the chart shows the heaviest person.

Cumulative frequency graph

This does exactly what it says on the tin. Frequency means 'how many' and 'cumulative' means to add up. So the chart below shows the total number of students achieving 'at least' a given mark.

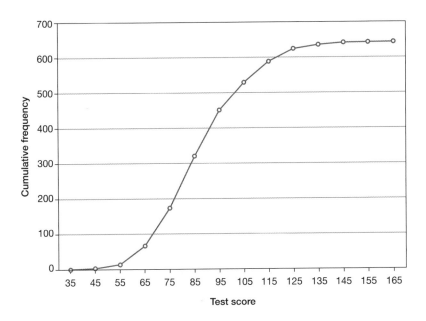

It shows that the lowest mark was 35 because that is where the curve starts. Reading off the Y axis, approximately 640 people took the test (this is where the curve finishes) and the top mark was 165. That is, everyone who took the test scored 165 or less. If 640 people took the test, the median mark will be at 320 (half of 640). This suggests that the median mark is 85 (reading across from 320).

Box and whisker plot

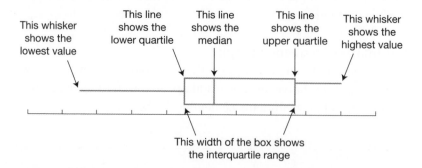

This whisker shows the lowest value

This line shows the lower quartile

This line shows the median

This line shows the upper quartile

This whisker shows the highest value

This width of the box shows the interquartile range

This is probably new to you. Many people panic a bit when they first see a box and whisker plot. There is no need to. They are very easy to read. The diagram above shows you how to read it. The line inside the box always shows you the 'median'. The lowest value can be read by looking at end of the left-hand whisker and the greatest value by looking at the top of the right-hand whisker.

50% of the data falls above and below the median. The distance between the end of the box and the end of the whisker shows the 'quartile range'. This means that a quarter or 25% of the data falls in this range.

The best way to explain how to use one is by looking at question 1 below.

Question 1

You give two classes you teach the same test. The box and whisker plot below shows the results for each class. The test was out of 60 marks. Indicate all the true statements.

A. The range of marks for class 2 was greater than class 1.

B. The median mark for class 2 was the same as for class 1.

C. In class 1 one quarter of the pupils achieved 40 or more.

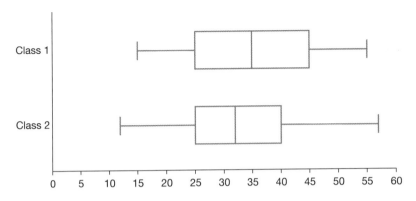

Answers:

Statement A is true: The range is the difference between the lowest mark and the highest mark.

Class 1: Lowest mark = 15, Highest mark = 55, so the range is 55 − 15 = 40

Class 2: Lowest mark = 12, Highest mark = 57, so the range is 57 − 12 = 45

Statement B is false: The median mark is shown by the line across the middle of the 'box', so:

Class 1 Median = 35; Class 2 Median = 32

Statement C is true: The length of the whisker above the box shows the achievement of the top 25% of the pupils. So, actually a quarter of the pupils achieved over 45 marks. So it must be true that a quarter of pupils achieved 40 marks or more.

Question 2

You carry out a science experiment with your class. The cumulative frequency diagram below shows the results. Indicate all the true statements.

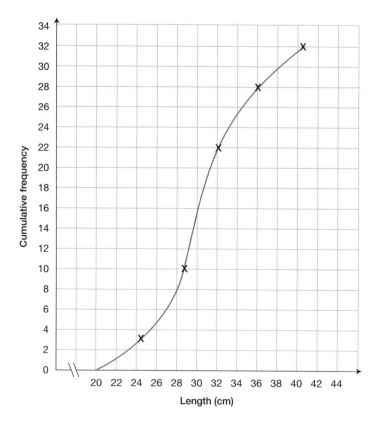

A. 30 pupils carried out the experiment.

B. The median length was 30 cm.

C. No pupils recorded a length greater than 32 cm.

Answers:

Statement A is false: The final point shows a 'cumulative frequency' of 32. That means that 32 pupils carried out the experiment altogether. It also shows that all the measurements were between 20 (the start of the curve) and 42 (the furthest point of the curve).

Statement B is true: We saw above that 32 pupils carried out the experiment. The median value is the 'middle' value, so we need to look at the curve to see the distance measured by the 16th pupil. This is 30 cm.

Statement C is false: When we discussed statement A, you saw that the longest value was 42 cm. The answer here is meant to 'trick' you because there are 32 pupils. Make sure you read off the correct scale or axis.

Question 3

As Head of Department, you are asked to interpret two pie charts of the GCSE results for your department over the last two years.

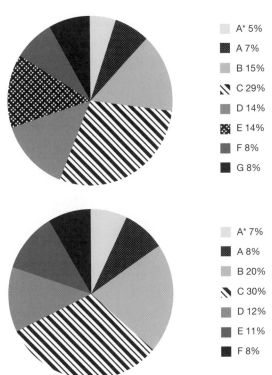

A* 5%
A 7%
B 15%
C 29%
D 14%
E 14%
F 8%
G 8%

A* 7%
A 8%
B 20%
C 30%
D 12%
E 11%
F 8%

Success in the written questions

1   By how many percentage points do the A* to C grades improve over the two years?

2   How many more pupils achieved an A or A* grade in the second year?

Calculation strategies

1   This is probably easiest to see in a table. I have copied the figures from the charts into the table below for the A* to C grades.

	A*	A	B	C	Total
Year 1	5	7	15	29	56
Year 2	7	8	20	30	65

65% pupils gained A* to C in year 2 compared with 56% in year 1. This is an increase of 9 percentage points. The pie charts show percentages and not individual pupils, so we can read this answer directly from the charts.

Answer: The grades improved by 9 percentage points.

2   12% of pupils gained an A or A* in year 1 (5% + 7%)

   15% of pupils gained an A or A* in year 2 (7% + 8%)

This does not mean that 6 more pupils achieved an A or an A* because these are percentages. We have to convert the percentages into pupils to find the answer.

In year 1, 75 students were entered, so we need to work out 12% of 75. To do this we calculate:

$$\frac{12}{100} \times 75 \ = \ 9 \text{ pupils} \quad (12\% \text{ is 12 out of 100, which is the same as } 12/100)$$

In year 2 the increase was 15% of 80 pupils, so we need to calculate:

$$\frac{15}{100} \times 80 = 12 \text{ pupils}$$

(I used the on-screen calculator for both these calculations.)

Answer: 3 more pupils achieved A* or A in the second year.

Question 4

Your colleague gives you a bar chart they have prepared that shows the percentage of pupils opting for GCSE subjects. There are 125 students in the year group. The maximum that can take drama is 24 because of the size of the studio. Will you need to reduce the size of the drama group?

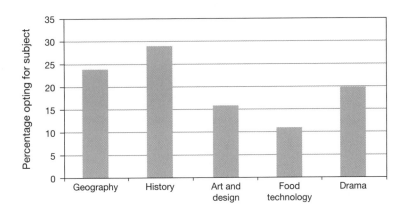

Calculation strategies

Reading the bar chart, 20% of the students opted for drama. So we need to find 20% of 125.

This is

$$\frac{20}{100} \times 125 = 25$$

You could actually have calculated this mentally. 10% of 125 is 12.5, so 20% is 25. Or you might recognise that 20% is the same as 1/5 and 1/5 of 125 is 25.

Answer: You need to reduce the size of the group by 1.

Question 5

The table below shows the results for 12 pupils in a mental mathematics test that they take each week.

Pupil	Test score			
A	10	13	13	15
B	11	13	15	17
C	14	14	13	15
D	18	19	18	19
E	9	13	15	17
F	14	16	15	16
G	16	16	16	17
H	12	14	15	17
I	20	19	18	20

What fraction of pupils showed a consistent trend of improvement? Give your answer as a fraction in its lowest form.

Calculation strategy

Three pupils consistently improve (that means their scores get better each week. It doesn't count as improvement if the score stays the same). There are 9 pupils altogether.

So the fraction is 3/9. We can cancel this down by dividing the numerator and the denominator by 3.

Answer: 1/3

Question 6

You teach in the modern languages department in a small school and your Head of Department shows you this scatter diagram representing pupils' marks in a French exam and a German exam.

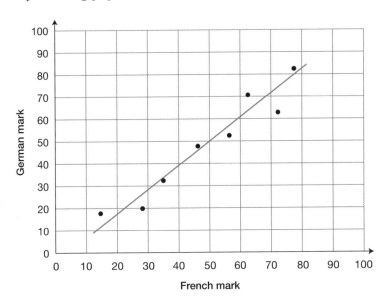

Which of the following statements are true?

A.   100 pupils took both the French and German exams.

B.   The highest French mark any pupil achieved was 78.

C.   If you score well in French you are unlikely to score well in German.

D.   The range of marks in the German exam is 63.

Answers

Each point on the chart represents one pupil. You can find out what mark they got in the German test by reading off the vertical axis. Similarly you can find out their French mark by reading off the horizontal axis.

Success in the written questions

Statement A is false: 8 pupils took both exams because there are 8 points plotted on the diagram.

Statement B is true: The scores on the French exam are read off the X axis (the horizontal line) and if we read down from the point furthest along the X axis it is at 78.

Statement C is false: The 'line of best fit' (the line that roughly goes through the middle of all the points) slopes upwards. This shows 'positive correlation', which means that the better you do in French, the better you do in German. You can also see this from looking at the marks. Never let mathematical terms put you off – just look at the information you are presented with. The answer will be there.

Statement D is true: Reading from the Y axis (the vertical line), the lowest mark is 18 and the highest is 81. So the range of marks is from 18 to 81 and we calculate it by calculating 81 – 18, which is 63.

Question 7

You need to find out the mean number of pupils in your school. Use the table below to calculate this. Give your answer to the nearest whole number.

Year group	Number of pupils
Reception	28
Year 1	31
Year 2	32
Year 3	27
Year 4	26
Year 5	29
Year 6	31

Calculation strategy

You calculate the mean using the following formula:

$$\frac{\text{Total number of pupils}}{\text{Number of classes}} = \frac{28 + 31 + 32 + 27 + 26 + 29 + 31}{7}$$

$$= \frac{204}{7}$$

$$= 29.14$$

Use a calculator to work this out. Remember there is an on-screen calculator. To the nearest whole number the answer is 29. Always remembering to ask 'Is the answer sensible?' Well, yes – it is!

Answer: 29 pupils

Using simple formulae

There is usually at least one question in the on-screen section that asks you to substitute numbers into a formula to carry out a calculation. This is something that might look complicated at first, but if you just follow a few simple steps these are easy marks to get.

It is easiest to illustrate this through two example questions.

Question 1

You set an English test and decide to weight the components of the test. The table below shows the components and the weighting.

Component	Weighting	Test marked out of
Spelling	20%	20
Speaking and listening	40%	20
Writing	40%	20

Success in the written questions

The formula you should use to calculate the total mark is:

Percentage mark = Spelling mark + 2 (Speaking and listening mark + Writing mark)

A pupil scores the following:

Spelling: 15/20

Speaking and listening: 18/20

Writing: 12/20

What is their final percentage mark?

Calculation strategies

Let's look at the formula you are given.

Percentage mark = Spelling mark + 2 (Speaking and listening mark + Writing mark)

Take the part 2(Speaking and listening mark + Writing mark). The 2 outside the bracket means that I add the two marks together and then double them.

So to find the answer put the scores into the formula:

$$\text{Percentage mark} = 15 + 2(18 + 12)$$
$$= 15 + 2 \times 30$$
$$= 15 + 60 = 75\%$$

Answer: 75%

Question 2

You are asked to send a sample of examination papers for moderation. The formula you are asked to apply is to send 1 paper for every 8 pupils at each level. You should always round the answer down. Complete the table below to show how many papers you will send.

Calculation strategies

This can be confusing because the formula asks you to round down. When we are rounding numbers, we always round up. The reason you are asked to round down in this case is to reduce the number of papers that the teachers need to moderate. Another example of having to read the questions carefully.

Grade	Number of pupils	Sample
A*	17	
A	22	
B	38	
C	48	

Divide the number of pupils in the table by 8.

Grade	Number of pupils	Sample
A*	17	2.125
A	22	2.75
B	38	4.75
C	48	6

Remember: the instruction was to round down each time. This is often the case in moderation to reduce the size of the sample.

Answer:

Grade	Number of pupils	Sample
A*	17	2
A	22	2
B	38	4
C	48	6

Success in the written questions

That is the on-screen test for you. I hope that you found that even the areas that were unfamiliar at first made sense when you had tried a few examples. Earlier in the book I suggested trying to make everyday use of facts and figures in the media. This is particularly true for the on-screen test because the bulk of it is about understanding and interpreting charts and diagrams. Look in the newspapers every day for the way they illustrate data – get yourself into the habit of interpreting these diagrams and charts and the test will be second nature! You will also be able to use interesting real-life examples in your classrooms to make mathematics come alive.

6 | Successful spelling

This chapter explains:

- The form that the spelling test will take.
- How phonics can help you with spelling, and the times that it doesn't.
- About vowels, consonants and spelling.
- The tips and rules that apply to spelling.

Be reassured about the spelling test. You will not be expected to know the spellings of words that are not in common usage or words used in a school context. Few people can claim to be perfect spellers (including the author of this chapter!) and it is unlikely you will be able to spell correctly all the words in the test. However, you can improve your spelling by following a few sensible guidelines. Do the diagnostic test below and if you get 25 or more right then you probably do not need to worry too much about the actual spelling test.

For the test you will use headphones. One word has been deleted from each sentence and when you reach this word, click the icon for Audio and listen. You will hear the deleted word. Decide how the word should be spelled and type your answer into the box provided. You can hear the word as many times as you like, but remember you have only a limited time to complete the tests and you cannot return to the spelling test once you have left it. For hearing-impaired students a multiple choice test such as the one in this book is used.

Diagnostic test

This list is to help you identify your strengths and weaknesses in spelling. Fifteen words are correct and fifteen are incorrect. Tick the correct spellings and correct the misspelled words. Where you are uncertain about the correct spelling, put a question mark.

1	accidentally	16	questionaire
2	beleive	17	seperate
3	accomodation	18	curriculum
4	embarrass	19	refered
5	commited	20	rhythm
6	parallel	21	queue
7	catagory	22	accessable
8	available	23	theater
9	definitely	24	testefy
10	guarantee	25	disappear
11	foriegn	26	calender
12	humourous	27	commitee
13	maintenance	28	forty
14	independent	29	freind
15	noticeable	30	interrupt

If you have spelled 25 or more of these words correctly, then you should not have a problem with the test. Check your answers in Appendix 6.1 at the end of the chapter.

- If you have got questions 1, 3, 4, 5, 6, 16, 18, 19, 25, 27 and 30 wrong, or you guessed correctly, read the section on double consonants.

- If you have got question 23 wrong, read the section on American spellings.

- If you have got questions 2 and 29 wrong, read the section on spelling tips for 'i before e'.

- If you have got questions 7, 9, 10, 11, 20, 26, 28 wrong, read the section on words to learn by heart.

- If you had problems with question 21, read the section on words with a 'q'.

- If you had problems with questions 8, 15, 22, read the section on words ending in *able* or *ible*.

- If you had problems with questions 13 and 14, read the section on words ending in *ance, ant, ence, ent* and learn by heart.

- If you had problems with question 12, read the section on words ending in *ous, ious, ary, ation, ific, ise, ize*.

- If you had problems with question 24, read the section on words ending in *efy* and *ify*.

Spelling and phonics

The vast majority of words are spelt as they sound. It can be useful to split up long and difficult words. For example, the word *dog* is made up of three individual sound units. However, many people find it difficult to identify different sounds and there is often more than one way to spell a sound. You may find it helpful to study the section below, but please do not depend on this approach for the spelling test.

Phonemes

In the table below are the 44 sounds (phonemes is the technical term for this) with some of the spelling options for each sound.

Phonemes table

Sound	Examples	Sound	Examples
/a/	rat	/g/	good, ghost, egg
/ae/	ape, bake, rain, steak, neighbourhood	/h/	half, wholemeal
/air/	tear, hare, hair	/j/	jeep, gentleman, rage, bridge
/ar/	jar, last	/l/	limp, tell, example, pupil
/e/	head, peg	/m/	make, hammer, climb
/ee/	meet, thief, reach, money	/n/	nod, runner, kneel, gnash
/i/	wanted, rig, cygnet	/ng/	sing, blink
/ie/	tried, my, fly, shine	/p/	path, happy
/o/	log, because	/kw/	quiz, queen
/oe/	cold, flow, want	/r/	rabbit, merry, wrong
/oi/	toy, boy	/s/	sun, mess, house, circle, mice
/oo/	book, would	/sh/	shoulder, permission, ration, chauffeur
/or/	torn, worn, door	/t/	top, better, doubt, missed
/ow/	shout, down, house	/th/	this, that, thunder
/u/	love, rough, tough		
/ur/	term, person, work	/v/	voice, leave
/ue/	grew, blue, moon	/w/	winter, whip
/b/	bottom, rabbit	/ks/gz/	box, exit
/c/k/	cook, key, quick, antique	/y/	yesterday
/ch/	chat, church, patch	/z/	zinc, jazz, sneeze, is, please
/d/	dot, bladder, rubbed	/zh/	pleasure, Asia, azure
/f/	fog, photo, cough, staff	/uh/	mutton, computer, conduit

Vowels and consonants

The vowels in English are *a* / *e* / *i* / *o* / *u*. All the other letters in the alphabet are called consonants. Every word in English must have at least one vowel.

Y is a vowel when it sounds like *i* or *e* (e.g. sly, dry, fry, why).

Words spelled with double consonants

These are probably the most difficult words to spell because you cannot rely on the sounds of letters to ensure you spell them correctly. The list below contains examples of words that often cause difficulty.

Three words are spelt incorrectly; correct them. Answers are at the end of the chapter in Appendix 6.2.

Accommodation	Curriculum	Occurrence
Aggressive	Deterrent	Opportunity
Allowed	Disappoint	Parrallel
Annually	Dissipate	Personnel
Aparatus	Disappearance	Permission
Appropriate	Embarrass	Preferrable
Approve	Finally	Questionnaire
Assess	Harass	Recommend
Balloon	Incidentally	Satellite
Committed	Millennium	Success
Committees	Necessary	Succinct
Coolly	Occasionally	Truthfully

American spellings

American spellings are *not* accepted in the test except that verbs ending in *ise* can be spelled *ize.*

Words that end in *re* in British English often end in *er* in American English:

British English	American English
Centre	Center
Fibre	Fiber
Litre	Liter
Theatre	Theater

Words that end in *our* in British English usually end in *or* in American English:

British English	American English
Colour	Color
Flavour	Flavor
Humour	Humor
Labour	Labor

Verbs ending in *ize* or *ise* in British English are always spelled with *ize* at the end in American English:

British English	American English
apologise *or* apologize	apologize
recognise *or* recognize	recognize

Verbs ending in *yse* in British English are always spelled *yze* in American English:

British English	American English
analyse	analyze
paralyse	paralyze

Words ending in a vowel plus *l* double the *l* when adding endings that begin with a vowel. In American English the *l* is not doubled:

British English	American English
Travel	Travel
Travelled	Traveled

Program or Programme? Program is the American spelling, but British English uses programme, unless referring to computers.

Commonly confused words

It is important to realise that the spelling of some words that can have similar sounds varies according to their function/meaning in a sentence. See the section at the end of Chapter 7, which gives information about parts of speech.

(a) **Accept** (verb) means to agree to receive or to do something:

> *She will accept her failure to master Japanese and will not take the examination again.*

Except (preposition) means to take or leave out:

> *Everything is on the shelves except dictionaries.*

(b) **Advice** (noun) means recommendations about what to do:

> *The advice from teachers was to study a foreign language.*

Advise (verb) means to recommend something:

> *He will advise her to study French.*

(c) **Affect** (verb) means to influence/to cause a change:

> *He will affect the way subjects are taught in schools.*

Effect (noun) means a result/consequence:

> *The important effect of changing the school start time was a real improvement in punctuality.*

(d) **Aisle** (noun) a passage between seats in a church or theatre:

> *The church aisle was crowded with prams during the service.*

Isle (noun) an island:

> *The Isle of Man is a popular holiday resort.*

(e) **Altogether** (adverb) means as a whole:

> *Altogether, the hockey team played well.*

All (pronoun) **together** (adverb) means everything in one place:

> *All together there were fifty people at the party.*

(f) **Assent** (noun) means agreement:

> *The assent of a majority of the population is needed at election time.*

Ascent (noun) means climb:

> *The ascent to the top of the mountain was difficult.*

(g) **Aural** (adjective) connected to hearing:

> *The aural test involves listening carefully to a short story and then answering the written questions about the main characters.*

Oral (adjective) connected to speaking:

> *The French oral test involves answering questions on a number of topics.*

(h) **Complement** (noun) the number required to make up a team, crew etc.:

> *The complement required for a hockey team is eleven.*

Compliment (noun) praise, admiration shown to someone:

> *The teacher was paid a generous compliment by the OFSTED inspector who thought her lesson was outstanding.*

(i) **Continuous** (adjective) means without a break:

The film was continuous from late afternoon to late evening.

Continual (adjective) means something that is persistent and frequently repeated:

The continual poor behaviour of pupils was a real problem for some staff.

(j) **Council** (noun) means a group that consults or advises:

The town council meets monthly to discuss local issues.

Counsel (verb) means to advise:

The teacher will counsel the sixth formers tomorrow on how to get the best out of a university course.

(k) **Disinterested** (adjective) means impartial:

He was disinterested in the result of the soccer match between Everton and Liverpool because he was a Manchester United supporter.

Uninterested (adjective) means bored:

He was uninterested at the soccer match because his local team was not involved.

(l) **Elicit** (verb) means to draw or bring out:

The teacher will elicit from the pupils the name of the person who was responsible for the graffiti in the toilets.

Illicit (adjective) means not permitted or illegal:

It was an illicit action to smuggle drugs into the United Kingdom.

(m) **Foreword** (noun) means an introduction to a written text:

The foreword to a novel often gives us information about the characters in the story.

Forward (adjective) describes who/what is in the front:

The forward party of six pupils and two staff started to climb the mountain first, leaving the rest of the group to follow.

(n) **Its** (possessive pronoun/possessive adjective) means of or belonging to it:

The child will cry when its mother is upset.

It's (a contraction for it is):

It's a day to celebrate when the examinations finish.

(o) **Imply** (verb) means suggest:

To imply that the teacher is wrong is not always a good idea.

Infer (verb) means to deduce:

To infer from the evidence that the motorist is guilty is probably correct.

(p) **Lose** (verb) means to no longer have:

To lose pupils on a school trip is not a good idea.

Loose (adjective) means not attached:

The pupils' satchels were loose on their shoulders.

(q) **Pores** (noun) means very small openings in the skin:

The patient had many pores in her skin.

Pore (verb) means to study something earnestly and carefully:

The students will pore over their notes before the examination.

Pour (verb) means to flow rapidly:

Water will pour out of the broken drainpipe.

(r) **Septic** (adjective) means infected:

   The bite wound turned septic after two days in the jungle.

   Sceptic (noun) means a person who will not accept anything without reliable proof:

   The sixth former was a sceptic who rejected religious beliefs.

(s) **Stationary** (adjective) means not moving:

   The bus was stationary at the end of the road.

   Stationery (noun) means writing materials:

   The school provided essential stationery items such as pens, pencils and paper.

(t) **Weather** (noun) means climatic conditions:

   The weather will be sunny tomorrow.

   Whether (conjunction) means an alternative possibility:

   We are going to the cricket match whether it rains or shines.

Spelling tips

Here are some useful rules (and exceptions) in English spelling. Use the information in the numbered sections to help you understand any mistakes you have made in the diagnostic and practice tests.

i before e except after c

ie	ei
believe	deceive
chief	receive
piece	perceive
mischief	ceiling
niece	
thief	

Successful spelling

Exceptions to the rule *i* before *e* except after *c* include words with a long *a* sound:

eight
veil
sleigh
reign

Homophones

Homophones are words that sound the same but are spelled differently and have different meanings:

air/heir	meet/meat
alright/all right	peace/piece
are/our	practice/practise/practical
bare/bear	real/reel
cent/scent	steel/steal
complement/compliment	tail/tale
die/dye	their/there
fair/fayre	to/too/two
hair/hare	waist/waste
hear/here	weak/week
knight/night	

Words ending in ance, ant, ence, ent

These are difficult to spell. Some tips are:

a) for people the ending is usually *ant*, e.g. serge*ant*, but exceptions include presid*ent* and resid*ent*

b) there are more words ending in *ent* or *ence* than in *ant* or *ance*.

English words containing the letter q are always followed by the vowel u

queue

acquaintance

frequent

questionnaire

Exceptions to this are words from other languages that are now commonly used in England, for example niqab (a veil worn by some Muslim women).

Words ending in able or ible

These endings are usually in adjectives meaning 'able to be . . .'. More often than not, when a word ends in *able* the main part of the word is a complete word in itself, e.g. read*able*, accept*able* and bear*able*.

Words ending in *ible*, with a few exceptions (see below), are incomplete without the *ible* ending, e.g. incred*ible* and feas*ible*.

However, inevitably, there are some exceptions, e.g. access*ible* and collaps*ible*, formed from the words access and collapse.

Adding ful or fully to words

Put simply, *ful* is used to form nouns or adjectives, e.g. a power*ful* politician, a skil*ful* player.

To form adverbs, the ending is always *-fully*, e.g. The school tennis team played success*fully* against their closest rivals.

Adding the endings ous, ious, ary, ation, ific, ise, ize

For nouns that end in *our*, you need to change the *our* to *or*:

hum*our*	hum*or*ous
lab*our*	lab*or*ious

Verbs ending in efy and ify

More verbs end with *ify* than *efy*. Examples include:

falsify, testify, modify, simplify, justify

However, there are four commonly used words that end in *efy*:

liquefy, stupefy, rarefy, putrefy

Words ending in ious and eous

These endings are used to form adjectives. Words ending with *ious* are far more common than those ending in *eous*.

Commonly used adjectives ending in *ious*:

ambitious, previous, conscious, glorious, obvious, studious, serious, tedious, various, religious, anxious, rebellious, superstitious.

Commonly used adjectives ending in *eous*:

courteous, miscellaneous, gorgeous, simultaneous, erroneous, gaseous.

fore or for?

If you are uncertain about whether to spell a word with *for* or *fore,* think about the meaning of the word.

for is normally used to convey the meaning of banning or giving up. For example:

forbid – refuse to allow
forfeit – give something up

Other commonly used words which begin with *for* are:

forgive, forget, forlorn, formality, fortunate

There are more words beginning with *fore* than those beginning with *for*. It means at or toward the front. Some of the most common words using *fore* are listed below:

> forehead, foreword, foretell, forefinger, foretaste, foreshadow, foresee, foreman

Forming plurals of words

Most nouns form plurals by adding an *s* to the singular form, e.g. *student, students*. However, a number of nouns ending in *f* or *fe* form the plural by changing the ending to *ve* before adding the *s*:

> loaf, loaves   knife, knives
>
> wolf, wolves   life, lives

Singular nouns ending in *s, sh, ch or x* form the plural by adding *es*:

> bus, buses   witch, witches
>
> fish, fishes   box, boxes

Plurals of singular nouns ending in *o*
If the *o* is preceded by a vowel it is usually correct to just add an *s*:

> video, videos, radio, radios

However, if the *o* is preceded by a consonant, the plural form is usually *es*:

> echo/echoes
>
> potato/potatoes

Words to learn by heart

These are some words in everyday use that do not conform to spelling rules and you just have to learn them:

absence	Mediterranean
acquire	mischievous
acquit	naive
appearance	noticeable
argument	occasion
benefited	perseverance
business	possess
calendar	precede
Caribbean	psychiatrist
category	questionnaire
coolly	reference
exceed	relevant
existence	rhyme
foreign	rhythm
forty	sceptic
guarantee	schedule
half	separate
halves	supersede
humour	twelfth
judgement	tyranny
liaison	vacuum
maintenance	weird
manoeuvre	

Practice test

The test questions will look something like this. Remember there are 10 marks for spelling. In the real test you will be asked to listen to the word and then type the correct spelling in the space in the sentence.

For this practice test just tick the correct spelling. The answers are in Appendix 6.3 at the end of this chapter. Please note that in the actual test you cannot return to this section once you have left it.

1 Most secondary schools today have _____ to involve pupils in decision making.

   commites comittes committees comitees

2 The science _____ was very difficult for Year 10 pupils.

   experement exparimant experiment experiment

3 The teacher decided to use an extract from a television _____ about the migration of birds.

   program programme programe progreme

4 It was an interesting _____ to teach pupils in single-sex groups for science.

   manoeuvre manoeuvre manaeouvre menoeuvre

5 The _____ for learning was first class in this comprehensive school.

   envaronment enviranment environment environmant

6 Teaching pupils about _____ in poetry is not as easy as the text books claim.

   rtyhm ryhthm rhytmh rhythm

7 The reign of Henry Tudor was taught in a _____ way by the trainee teacher.

   curious curios curieus corious

Successful spelling

8 The school _____ was responsible for collecting the money for the school trip to the Lake District.

secretery secratary secretary secratery

9 We would not _____ going to all-night parties the night before you start teaching.

recomend recommend reccommend recommand

10 The school _____ was extended to include Saturday mornings.

weak wiek week weke

11 Reading tests are taken _____ by primary school pupils.

anually annualy annuelly annually

12 All the Year 12 pupils will _____ in their examinations.

succeed succede succed succade

13 It was agreed _____ that the school summer holiday should begin after the end of July.

unanimously unanimouslly unenimously unenimosly

14 It is _____ that absence in Year 11 has been so high this academic year.

regretrable regretible regrettable regrattable

15 Teaching _____ is demanding but very enjoyable.

prectice practise practice practese

16 The _____ for school dinners gets longer week by week.

qeueu queue quewe qeeue

17 The school's low-attaining pupils _____ from the pupil premium.

benefitted benifited benefited benifted

18 Parents were _____ to the changes to school uniform.

agreable agreeable aggreable agreeible

19 Pupils in Year 9 are _____ rather than nasty.

misceivous mischavious mischeivous mischievous

20 _____ is a key factor in learning new ideas and concepts.

perseverance persaverence perseveranse perseverennce

21 The school drama group performed _____ at the regional final.

sucessfully successfuly succesfully successfully

22 Members of staff at this school are very _____

conscientious concientious consciencious conscentious

23 Most people _____ some words

misspel mispell misspell mispel

24 The school _____ spend a lot of time observing teaching and learning.

hiarachy heirarchy hierarchy hiarechy

25 _____ trips are valuable educational experiences for pupils of all ages.

theatre theater theatar thaetre

I hope that the diagnostic test and the final test that you have just carried out have shown you that you can pass the spelling part of the literacy test with confidence. More importantly you should have become better at spelling in everyday life, which will make you a better model for the pupils that you teach. It may have even made you more confident in your own writing.

The next area to revise is grammar.

Appendix 6.1

Answers to diagnostic spelling test with correct spellings:

1	correct	16	incorrect: questionnaire
2	incorrect: believe	17	incorrect: separate
3	incorrect: accommodation	18	correct
4	correct	19	incorrect: referred
5	incorrect: committed	20	correct
6	correct	21	correct
7	incorrect: category	22	incorrect: accessible
8	correct	23	incorrect: theatre
9	correct	24	incorrect: testify
10	correct	25	correct
11	incorrect: foreign	26	incorrect: calendar
12	incorrect: humorous	27	incorrect: committee
13	correct	28	correct
14	correct	29	incorrect: friend
15	correct	30	correct

Appendix 6.2

The three words spelled incorrectly in the double consonants list are:

Aparatus should be apparatus.

Parrallel should be parallel.

Preferrable should be preferable.

Appendix 6.3

Spelling practice test answers and key points:

1   *committees* See section on double consonants and remember the double *e* vowel in this commonly misspelled word.

2   *experiment* Often pronounced 'ex-peer-a-mint'. Remember the *ment* ending.

3   *programme* American English always uses 'program' but British English always uses 'programme', unless referring to computers.

4   *manoeuvre* A difficult word and one to learn by heart.

5   *environment* Remember the *iron* bit and the *ent* ending.

6   *rhythm* Often spelled incorrectly and one to learn by heart.

7   *curious* Often misspelled with an *e* instead of *i*.

8   *secretary* Often misspelled with an *e* rather than an *a*. The first two vowels are *e* and the third is an *a*.

9   *recommend* See section on double consonants.

10 *week* See last example in section on homophones.

11 *annually* See spelling tip on adding *ful* or *fully* to words.

12 *succeed* Remember double consonant (*c*) and double vowel (*e*).

13 *unanimously* Remember the ending has only one *l* and a *u* before the *s*.

14 *regrettable* Remember the double consonant *t* and the *able* ending.

15 *practice* Practice is a noun, as in 'football practice' or 'teaching practice'. Practise is a verb, as in 'I practise playing the piano every Tuesday.'

16 *queue* See spelling tips on 'English words containing the letter *q* are always followed by the vowel *u*'.

17 *benefited* A word to learn by heart.

Successful spelling

18 *agreeable* See section on words ending with *ible* or *able.*

19 *mischievous* Remember the *i* before *e* rule except after *c.*

20 *perseverance* Remember all the vowels are *e*'s except for the *a* in the *ance* ending.

21 *successfully* See section on double consonants.

22 *conscientious* See spelling tips on words ending in *ious* and *eous.*

23 *misspell* See section on double consonants.

24 *hierarchy* Remember the rule '*i* before *e* except after *c*'.

25 *theatre* See section on American spellings.

7 Using grammar effectively

This chapter explains:

- What the grammar tests look like.
- The knowledge you will be tested on.
- The information you need to pass the grammar test successfully.

For grammar, 8–12 marks are awarded. You will be tested on your ability to understand and use written standard English and to communicate clearly to readers of your work in an educational context. You will need to demonstrate knowledge and accuracy in implementing the rules of English grammar. The test will also examine your ability to write for specific audiences, such as pupils, parents and governors.

Language is constantly changing but you will have to conform to what is generally acceptable. Dialect words such as 'owt' meaning 'anything' or 'nowt' meaning 'nothing' are likely to confuse people who are not used to listening to people with northern accents!

English teachers are expected to use standard forms to write pupil reports and comment on pupils' written work. For the test you will have to answer questions on a piece of writing about 8 to

12 sentences long. The texts could include extracts from government reports, pupils' reports and letters home to parents. Within the document there are gaps in the text with four options to fill the blank; only one option is correct.

Specifically, you will be tested on some of the following elements of grammatical knowledge:

1   failure to observe sentence boundaries

2   abandoned or faulty constructions and sentence fragments

3   lack of cohesion

4   lack of agreement between subject and verb

5   should have/of, might have/of

6   inappropriate or incomplete verb forms

7   wrong or missing preposition, e.g. different from/than/to

8   noun/pronoun agreement error

9   determiner/noun agreement error

10   inappropriate or missing determiner

11   problems with comparatives and superlatives

12   problems with relative pronouns in subordinate clauses

13   inappropriate or missing adverbial forms.

If you are uncertain about the terms used to describe key parts of speech, such as verbs, nouns and pronouns, then go to Appendix 7.3 where these will be explained.

Diagnostic test

The aim of this test is to find out your weaknesses (and strengths) in English grammar. Correct the mistakes in the sentences below. Answers are at the end of this chapter in Appendix 7.1. Please tick the one sentence that is correct:

1   The school teachers know my strengths and weaknesses, they have observed my lessons on teaching practice and they think I will be a good teacher.

2   Teachers work hard at school. They deserve long holidays.

3   It was too good a chance to miss, there are not many schools where you get the opportunity to teach sixth formers.

4   Worried about falling standards in the school so the headteacher called in heads of department to ask them to set pupils more homework.

5   Even though the school decided to ban mobile phones. History teachers are using them.

6   A teacher should get the support of parents even if they are struggling to mark pupils' work.

7   Good examination results was the major concern for schools.

8   Some pupils might of truanted from school today.

9   Most of the pupils had decided leave school early.

10 The behaviour of pupils in Year 2 was quite different than Year 11.

Failure to observe sentence boundaries

To be correct a sentence must contain a *subject*, which tells us what the sentence is about, and a *predicate*, which tells us about the subject: *The lively Year 10 group* (subject) *caused teachers a lot of problems* (predicate).

A *clause* is a group of words containing a subject and predicate. Main (independent clauses) can stand alone as complete sentences, e.g. *the pupils are hardworking.* Subordinate (dependent) clauses cannot stand alone but must be connected to a main clause: *Year 11 pupils are keen to do well* (main), *so teachers need to set them homework every week* (subordinate). In other words, a subordinate clause gives more information about the main clause.

107

Using grammar effectively

There are three types of sentence:

(a) Simple sentences have just one main clause and no subordinate clause:

> *The new school will open in September.*

(b) Compound sentences have two or more main clauses and no subordinate clause. The clauses can be linked by a conjunction or a semicolon:

> *I have problems with French grammar and I need a text book to check the accuracy of my work.*
>
> *Teachers always talk about school; they can dominate the conversation at parties.*

(c) Complex sentences consist of one main clause and at least one subordinate clause:

> *The school soccer team plays* (main clause) *when* (conjunction) *they have enough players to field a team* (subordinate clause).
>
> *The school soccer team plays* (main clause) *when* (conjunction) *they have enough players to field a team* (subordinate clause) *and* (conjunction) *the pitch is fit* (subordinate clause).

A major problem for many students is deciding when a sentence should end. What this means is that commas are sometimes used instead of full stops. As a general rule of thumb it is better to write shorter sentences instead of long complicated ones where the meaning may become confused and obscured. For example:

> *I have planned a lesson on First World War poetry for Year 9, this decision was influenced by my knowledge of these pupils who are very mature, I think they will enjoy the poems because the feelings expressed are so powerful.*

should be:

I have planned a lesson on First World War poetry for Year 9. This decision was influenced by my knowledge of these pupils who are very mature. I think they will enjoy the poems because the feelings expressed are so powerful.

Read about commas and full stops in the punctuation section. If you are uncertain about whether to use a comma or a full stop then use a full stop.

Abandoned or faulty constructions and sentence fragments

Abandoned and faulty constructions usually occur when sentences are long and complicated.

(a) Faulty construction

Overjoyed about the GCSE results so the headteacher gave permission to the pupils to leave school early to attend the pop concert in town.

This should read:

The headteacher, overjoyed about the GCSE results, gave permission to the pupils to leave school early to attend the pop concert in town.

It is this second sentence that makes it clear that it is the headteacher who is overjoyed about the GCSE results.

(b) Sentence fragment

In speech we use fragments all the time but they are not acceptable in writing. Some examples are shown below:

Most English universities offer a range of science courses. Such as Chemistry, Physics and Biology.

Possible revision:

Most English universities offer a range of science courses, such as Chemistry, Physics and Biology.

109

Using grammar effectively

Below are examples of incomplete sentences that cannot stand alone:

Teachers are sometimes blamed by politicians for poor pupil behaviour. Which isn't fair.

Homework is set regularly at most secondary schools. Very unpopular with students.

Until there is a staff meeting about the training day. The headteacher will not be able to decide upon the topic for discussion.

These examples are clearly not complete sentences and full stops are used incorrectly. They should probably read:

Teachers are sometimes blamed by politicians for poor pupil behaviour, which isn't fair.

Homework is set regularly at most secondary schools and is very unpopular with students.

Until there is a staff meeting about the training day, the headteacher will not be able to decide upon the topic for discussion.

Lack of cohesion

Put simply, cohesion means that a piece of writing appears as a single unit and not a random sequence of thoughts or sentences. One common cohesive device is the backward reference to something mentioned before. See the examples below.

(a) Use of pronouns to refer back to a noun:

My son is on the telephone. He says he needs the computer that he lent us.

(b) Use of the definite article to modify a noun that has been introduced with the indefinite article:

When I went to the bank on Wednesday I saw a male clerk and a female manager. The male clerk was unhelpful but the female manager gave me some good advice.

(c) Use of ellipsis (the omission of words that the reader will be able to supply mentally):

I want to go to the soccer match but I haven't the time to ... (go to the soccer match)

(d) Conjunctions such as *but, however, so, consequently* can be used to make pieces of writing cohesive.

I will start revising next week so I cannot go out in the evenings.

(e) This next short passage lacks cohesion.

A student teacher will enjoy teaching practice if there is good support from the school. They will find it difficult if the school is about to be inspected.

The noun *teacher* is singular but the pronoun it refers to, *they*, is plural. This is a common mistake but it can be rectified by careful proof reading. Does the sentence mean that the school and the student will find it 'difficult' if the school is to be inspected or just the student?

The sentence should probably read:

A student teacher will enjoy teaching practice if there is good support from the school. He or she will find it difficult if the school is about to be inspected.

Lack of agreement between subject and verb

This is a mistake many students and teachers make. Common mistakes include:

- two or more nouns (e.g. inspectors and advisers) with a singular verb (e.g. is)

- singular determiner (e.g. my) with a plural verb (e.g. were)
- plural determiner (e.g. those) with a singular verb (e.g. is).

Words that can cause problems for students are: *criterion* (singular) and *criteria* (plural) and *data,* which in common usage is singular, although it is sometimes used as a plural.

Two or more nouns with a singular verb

The judgements of the inspection team was positive about the hard-working staff and dedicated pupils.

This should be:

The judgements of the inspection team were positive about the hard-working staff and dedicated pupils.

Indefinite pronouns such as *everyone, nobody* and *anyone* require singular verbs.

But

Some indefinite pronouns such as *all* and *some* can be singular or plural, depending on what they are referring to:

Some of the students are in the assembly hall.

All of the equipment is missing.

Basic rule

A singular subject (*teacher, pupil, parent*) always takes a singular verb (*is, goes, plays*) and a plural subject (*teachers, pupils, parents*) always takes a plural verb (*are, go, play*). This sounds easy but there are some difficulties that you might encounter.

(a) The subject of a sentence will come before a phrase beginning with *of*:

Incorrect – *A library of non-fiction books are inadequate for pupils in secondary schools.*

Correct – *A library of non-fiction books is inadequate for pupils in secondary schools.*

(b) Two singular subjects connected by *either/or* or *neither/nor* need a singular verb:

Neither Mr Jones nor Ms Johnson is available to teach today.

Either Sally or David is helping with the school play.

(c) Two nouns with a singular verb:

Good university degree results was influenced by high-quality staff teaching and students' hard work.

This should read:

Good university degree results were influenced by high-quality staff teaching and students' hard work.

(d) Generally, you should use a plural verb with two or more subjects when they are connected by *and*:

English and French are important subjects in most schools.

(e) With words that indicate portions (*some, per cent, half* etc.), if the noun after *of* is singular, then use a singular verb. If it is plural, use a plural verb. For example,

A quarter of the student population has passed the course.

Twenty-five per cent of the students have passed the course.

(f) Singular verb with some non-English plurals, e.g. *criterion* (singular) and *criteria* (plural).

Data is now seen as a plural form.

Should have/of, might have/of

In English we use a lot of modal verbs like *can, could, may, might, must, ought to, shall, should, will, would* followed by the verb *have*. In speech it is perfectly acceptable to contract *should have* to *should've,* but try to avoid doing this in your writing. Remember it is always right to use *have*.

Should have refers to something that happened in the past, for example we *should have gone to the theatre last week.*

Remember it is incorrect to write:

I might of gone out last night but it started to rain.

The correct version is: *I might have gone out last night but it started to rain.*

Inappropriate or incomplete verb forms

These mistakes usually occur because a text has not been proof read carefully. Most of these errors can be avoided.

Most teachers are trained teach all year groups.

The correct version is:

Most teachers are trained to teach all year groups.

Remember all sentences must have a verb.

Many pupils in this school French and English.

This could read:

Many pupils in this school are French and English.

Or it could read:

Many pupils in this school like French and English.

Wrong or missing preposition, e.g. different from/than/to

Commonly used prepositions are words like *in, on, with, until, upon, since, by,* etc. There are a huge number of prepositions which, by and large, indicate the relationship among the various parts of a sentence.

Children arrive home by the end of the afternoon and are very tired.

Different from is viewed as correct in both British and American English. Use this form in your writing rather than *different than/to,* as in the following example.

Teachers are different from other workers because they talk about pupils all the time.

Noun/pronoun agreement

If you substitute a pronoun for a noun you have to use the correct pronoun so that the reader understands which noun you are referring to

(a) Agree the number

Put simply, if the pronoun replaces a singular noun then you will need a singular pronoun.

If a pupil misbehaves, he or she must be made aware of the consequences. Correct

If a pupil misbehaves, they must be made aware of the consequences. Incorrect

(b) Agree the person

If you are writing in the second person (you) do not confuse the reader by switching to the first person (I). This is the case if you switch from third person (he, she, it, etc.) to the first or second person.

Using grammar effectively

> *When a student attends tutorials, he or she should arrive on time.* Correct

> *When a student attends tutorials, you should arrive on time.* Incorrect

Remember that nouns remain the same no matter where they occur in sentences. Pronouns, however, do change a lot as demonstrated below in the following table:

First person singular:	I	me	my	mine	myself
Second person singular:	you	you	your	yours	yourself
Third person singular:	he/she	him/her	his/hers	his/hers	him/herself
	it	it	its	its	itself
First person plural:	we	us	our	ours	ourselves
Second person plural:	you	you	your	yours	yourselves
Third person plural:	they	them	their	theirs	themselves

I or *me*: use *I* when it is either the subject or part of the subject of a sentence. For example:

> *Ted, Rose and I went to the restaurant.*

Use *me* when it is the object or part of the object of a sentence. For example:

> *Ted went to the restaurant with Rose and me.*

Determiner/noun agreement error

Determiners are words like *this, that, these, those, the, a, an*. Mistakes can sometimes occur when the determiner is linked to its noun, for example:

This football games are on Saturday.

This should read:

These football games are on Saturday.

In this case the subject of the sentence is plural and requires a plural verb.

The following subjects of sentences can cause problems:

Examples of a novel

Kinds of milk

These two subjects above require a plural verb as shown below:

Most examples of a romantic novel includes a strong plot and interesting characters. Incorrect

Most examples of a romantic novel include a strong plot and interesting characters. Correct

Most kinds of milk is good for children. Incorrect

Most kinds of milk are good for children. Correct

Inappropriate or missing determiner

Determiners such as *this* and *that* are used with singular or uncountable nouns. *These* and *those* are used with plural nouns. *This/these* refer to something close at hand and *that/those* refer to something further away.

That school in the next county was very academic (a distance away)

This equipment is difficult to use (close at hand)

These pupils in our school are hard working (close at hand)

Those pupils in schools in the next town are lazy (a distance away)

Comparatives and superlatives

We use comparative adjectives to describe people and objects:

Jack is better at drawing than Jill.

We need to get a bigger classroom.

Than is used when we want to compare one thing with another:

Oliver is better than me at football.

To make comparisons in standard English we add *er* to adjectives such as *fresh/fresher* or start with *more* as in *more successful.*

In the Year 5 class girls worked harder than boys and were more motivated.

Superlatives are used to describe the ultimate in something:

The best student in the school is in Year 6.

Superlatives are used when three or more things are being compared and comparatives when only two things are compared:

Emily is the fittest twin.

should read

Emily is the fitter twin.

NB You are comparing two people.

Relative pronouns in subordinate clauses

If you start a sentence with a main clause, as below,

Year 8 pupils are difficult to teach

you may want to add information in a subordinate clause as to what you intend to do about this:

Year 8 pupils are difficult to teach so I will plan their lessons carefully.

The subordinate clause '*so I will plan their lessons carefully*' has a subject *I* and a verb *will plan*, but without the main clause it does not make complete sense.

Relative pronouns are sometimes used to start subordinate clauses, although most subordinate clauses start with conjunctions (connectives) such as *because, and, if, although* etc. The relative pronouns are: *who, whom, which, that.*

Examples of usage:

The soccer manager needed a player who could score goals.

The University Senate decided to appoint the lecturer whom the professor supported.

The new headteacher outlined the plans which had been agreed with the Governing Body.

The decision of the meeting was one that received the complete support of all governors.

In many cases it is possible to omit the relative pronoun, for example:

He was the teacher whom the governors wanted.

This could be written without the *whom* and also by replacing *whom* with *that*. Both these versions would be correct.

A common error students make is to use an inappropriate relative pronoun. The relative pronoun *which* is used when referring to inanimate things. For example:

Last year, the pupils achieved results which were the best in the school's history.

However, in the sentence below *which* is used incorrectly because footballers are not inanimate:

The England manager chose footballers which had played for the team before.

It should read:

The England manager chose footballers who had played for the team before.

Inappropriate or missing adverbial forms

This occurs when adjectives are used instead of adverbs. Native users of the language are unlikely to make this mistake, but non-native speakers may fall into this trap:

By and large, pupils in this school were taught sensitive (adjective).

This should read:

By and large, pupils in this school were taught sensitively (adverb).

Some words such as *fast* can be used as an adverb or adjective:

He is a fast (adjective) *runner.*

He can run fast (adverb).

Practice test

For the questions below tick the one sentence that seems to you to be the most appropriate in terms of grammatical accuracy. Answers are at the end of this chapter in Appendix 7.2.

Question 1

(a) Playing games at school helps pupils to develop their social skills and it is important in their development.

(b) Playing games at school helps pupils to develop their social skills and they are important in their development.

(c) Playing games at school helps a pupil to develop their social skills and they are important in their development.

(d) Playing games at school helps a pupil to develop his social skills, it is important in their development.

Question 2

At this primary school the day starts with an assembly.

(a) The pupils enjoy their morning assembly, singing the same songs as usual.

(b) Pupils were singing the same songs as usual, they enjoyed their morning assembly.

(c) Singing the same songs as usual, the pupils enjoyed their morning assembly.

(d) They enjoyed their morning assembly, singing the same songs as usual.

Questions 3–5

Read the following extract from a letter to pupils about school trips. For questions 3–5, tick the correct wording (a), (b), (c) or (d).

Using grammar effectively

Dear Pupils,

At the end of term there will be a number of educational visits for all year groups.

Question 3

The Art teachers

(a) is going to the National Gallery.

(b) were going to the National Gallery.

(c) will go to the National Gallery.

(d) shall go to the National Gallery.

Question 4

We are planning to take pupils

(a) which have chosen to take pottery next year.

(b) who has chosen to take pottery next year.

(c) whom has chosen to take pottery next year.

(d) who have chosen to take pottery next year.

Question 5

These visits will be for a full day and we will require a financial contribution from parents/carers before the trips, so make sure that

(a) you ask your parents/carers before you apply.

(b) you ask your parents/carers to apply.

(c) you ask your parents/carers too apply.

(d) you ask your parents/carers after you apply.

Yours sincerely,

James Rowlinson
Headteacher

Question 6

Read the following extract from a letter to parents and tick the most appropriate answer.

Dear Parents/Guardians,

Your son/daughter is about to enter Year 9.

(a) In the next academic year, the school offered a range of options for Year 9 pupils.

(b) In the next academic year, the school offers a range of options for Year 9 pupils.

(c) In the next academic year, the school will offer a range of options for Year 9 pupils.

(d) In the next academic year, the school has offered a range of options for Year 9 pupils.

Question 7

Tick the sentence which is correct.

(a) Although John had wanted to go to university to study English, his examination results is poor and it meant being more realistic about the courses he could study.

(b) Although John had wanted to go to university to study English, his examination results was poor and it meant being more realistic about the courses he could study.

(c) Although John wants to go to university to study English, his examination results were poor and they mean being more realistic about the courses he can study.

(d) Although John will want to go to study English, his examination results was poor and they mean being more realistic about the courses he can study.

Using grammar effectively

Question 8

(a) The problem with teaching Year 11 are that for long periods they cannot concentrate.

(b) The problems with teaching Year 11 is that for long periods they cannot concentrate.

(c) The problem with teaching Year 11 is that for long periods they cannot concentrate.

(d) The problems with teaching Year 11 are that for long periods they cannot concentrate.

Question 9

(a) Considering they were the most academic pupils in the school, the Head of English was surprised how poor their written work was.

(b) Considering they was the most academic pupils in the school, the poor quality of their written work was a surprise to the Head of English.

(c) Considering they were the most academic pupils in the school, it was surprising to the Head of English about the poor quality of their written work.

(d) The Head of English was surprised by the poor quality of their written work considering they were the most academic pupils in the school.

Question 10

(a) The school's annual Speech Night will be held this year on the 25th September. This is our annual event to celebrate pupils' achievements.

(b) The school's annual Speech Night is to be held this year on the 25th September. This will be are event to celebrate pupils' achievements.

c) The school's Speech Night will be held this year on the 25th September. This will be our annual event to celebrate pupils' achievements.

124

(d) The school's annual Speech Night will be held annually this year on the 25th September. This will be an event to celebrate pupils' achievements.

Question 11

(a) Music students practice on the piano every week.

(b) Music students practise on the piano every week.

(c) Music students have practiced on the piano every week.

(d) Music students will practice on the piano every week.

Question 12

(a) The best student in Year 11 is Hassan Ali.

(b) The better student in Year 11 is Hassan Ali.

(c) Hassan Ali is the better student in Year 11.

(d) In Year 11 Hassan Ali is the better student.

Question 13

(a) The school could of taken the pupils to the new Art gallery.

(b) The school should of taken the pupils to the new Art gallery.

(c) The school might of taken the pupils to the new Art gallery.

(d) The school could have taken the pupils to the new Art gallery.

Question 14

(a) The bus was stationery at the end of the road.

(b) The stationery bus was at the end of the road.

(c) The bus was stationary at the end of the road.

(d) The bus at the end of the road will be stationery.

Question 15

(a) The French pupils will be coming to are school today.

(b) The French pupils will be using our minibus during their stay.

(c) The French pupils will join or classes for all subjects.

(d) The French pupils will be sharing all are school facilities.

Appendix 7.1

Answers to the Diagnostic Test

1. *The school teachers know my strengths and weaknesses. They have observed my lessons on teaching practice and they think I will be a good teacher.*

   These are two separate sentences which cannot be joined by a comma. Read the section on sentence boundaries. As a general rule it is a good idea to write shorter sentences joined with conjunctions if you want to strengthen the relationship between the two sentences. For example: *The school teachers know my strengths and weaknesses because they have observed my lessons on teaching practice and they think I will be a good teacher.*

2. This is correct. There are two separate statements which have not been joined.

3. *It was too good a chance to miss. There are not many schools where you get the chance to teach sixth formers.*

   As with question 1, there should be two separate sentences unless you decide to link them with a conjunction.

4. This is an example of faulty construction. It should read:

   Worried about falling standards in the school, the headteacher called in heads of department to ask them to set pupils more homework.

   It is the *headteacher* who is worried about *falling standards.*

5. *Even though the school decided to ban mobile phones* is a sentence fragment. It does not make complete sense on its own. The sentence could read:

   Even though the school decided to ban mobile phones, History teachers are using them.

6. This is an example of lack of cohesion. There is a lack of agreement between the subject of the sentence *teacher* (singular) and the pronoun it refers to *they* (plural). The sentence should read:

    A teacher should get the support of parents even if he or she is struggling to mark pupils' work.

7. This is an example of the lack of agreement between the subject of the sentence, *examination results*, which is plural, and the verb *was*, which is singular. The sentence should read:

    Good examination results were the major concern for schools.

8. The sentence should read:

    Some pupils might have truanted from school today.

    Read the section on might of/might have.

9. The sentence should read:

    Most of the pupils had decided to leave school early.

    It does not make sense without the use of the preposition *to*.

10. The sentence should read:

    either: *The behaviour of pupils in Year 2 was quite different from Year 11.*

    or: *The behaviour of pupils in Year 2 was quite different to Year 11.*

    Different than is considered to be non-standard English.

Appendix 7.2

Answers to the Practice Test

Question 1

The only correct answer is (b) because *'they'* and *'their'* are plural to agree with *'games/pupils'*.

Using grammar effectively

Question 2
The correct answer is (a). The subject of the sentence is about the *pupils'* enjoyment of morning assembly because they were *singing the same songs as usual.*

Question 3
The correct answer is (c). This event is planned for the future by *'art teachers'* (plural) and requires a plural verb in the future tense *'will go'*.

Question 4
The correct answer is (d). See the section on the use of relative pronouns and when to use *who, whom, which,* etc.

Question 5
(a) is correct because *'before'* is the appropriate preposition.

Question 6
The correct answer is (c). The options for Year 9 are to be offered in the future.

Question 7
The correct answer is (c). This is an example of subject and tense inconsistency. *Examination results* is plural and needs a plural verb (*were*) and a plural pronoun (*they*) to be correct. John *wants* (present tense) to go to university and his *examination results* were in the past.

Question 8
The correct answer is (c). *Problem* is a singular noun requiring a singular verb *is* and *problems* is a plural noun requiring a plural verb *are.*

Question 9
The correct answer is (d). The subject of the sentence is the Head of English who is surprised about the poor quality of the pupils' written work.

Question 10

The correct answer is (c). In (a) and (d) *annual/annually* is repeated unnecessarily. In (b) *are* should be *our*.

Question 11

The correct answer is (b). *Practice* is a noun and *practise* is the verb.

Question 12

The correct answer is (a). *Better* is used to compare two things and *best* when three or more things are compared.

Question 13

The correct answer is (d). See the section on the use of modal verbs.

Question 14

The correct answer is (c). *Stationery* with an *e* means writing materials and *stationary* with an *a* means not moving.

Question 15

(b) is the correct answer because *our* is the appropriate personal pronoun. *Are* is a verb and *or* is a conjunction. These words are often confused because they sound similar but they are completely different in meaning.

Appendix 7.3

Key parts of speech

ADJECTIVES

An adjective tells us more about a noun. For example, *an intelligent student, a yellow submarine* and *an expensive car.*

ADVERBS

An adverb gives us more information about a verb but can also be used to modify adjectives and other adverbs. Adverbs tell us when, where and how something takes place. They usually but, not always, end in *ly*: *Peter played quietly. Fast* is often used as an adverb: *John runs fast.*

Using grammar effectively

CONJUNCTIONS

Words such as *and, but, because* and *or*. They are used primarily to join words, phrases and clauses: *We could go to the cinema or watch the television.*

DETERMINERS

These are words used with nouns to help define them, for example, *this library book, the pupils, twenty teachers*. They include: the indefinite and definite articles (*a/an* and *the*)

NOUNS AND PRONOUNS

Nouns are probably the most important words for conveying meaning. Children learn to use nouns to get what they want before they start to use pronouns or even verbs. Understanding a passage with the nouns removed is extremely difficult.

Put simply nouns are naming words and there are different types of nouns:

PROPER NOUNS

They always begin with a capital letter and refer to something which is concrete and specific:

- Names of people: 'William Shakespeare', 'Charlie Chaplin' and 'Winston Churchill'.

- Names of places: 'London', 'Tate Modern' and 'Wembley Stadium'.

- Names of occasions: 'Ramadan', 'Christmas Day' and other religious events. Public holidays such as 'New Year's Day'.

- Names of films, books, newspapers etc.: 'The Guardian', 'Star Wars' and 'Sons and Lovers'.

- Names of events: 'Golcar Lily Day', 'Pennine Spring Music Festival' and 'Speech Day'.

COMMON NOUNS

Common nouns describe objects and they do not have a capital letter. For example: car, book and school. They can be further classified into:

Abstract nouns – things you cannot see or touch, e.g. happiness and courage.

Collective nouns – words which describe groups, e.g. team and choir. You should treat collective nouns as being singular.

Compound nouns – nouns made up of more than one word, e.g. drinks tray and water bottle.

Concrete nouns – things you can see or touch, e.g. clouds and cats.

NOUN PHRASE

A noun phrase is a group of words that perform as a noun. It could be replaced by a pronoun: *The first female headteacher of the school.* This phrase could be replaced with *she.*

PRONOUNS

Pronouns are substitutes for nouns and are used to avoid repetition. For example,

Personal pronouns
I/me, you/you, he/him

Possessive pronouns
My/mine, your/yours

Reflexive pronouns
Myself, herself, ourselves

Interrogative pronouns
These are used in questions: who/whom, what, which.

PREPOSITIONS

These are linking words which can be used to connect a noun with another noun (or noun phrase) or to connect verbs. Commonly used prepositions: *by, at, with, near, from.*

Using grammar effectively

VERBS

These are words which describe what we do or what we are. Verbs can express:

A physical action	to *swim*, to *dance*, to *throw*
A mental action	to *think*, to *reflect*, to *ponder*
A state of being	to *be*, to *exist*, to *appear*.

Active verbs and Passive verbs

Active verbs tell us what someone did: *Miriam stopped teaching the class when the bell went for the end of school.*

Passive verbs tell us what was done to someone: *Miriam was stopped from teaching the class when the bell went for the end of school.*

Auxiliary verbs

The main ones are *do, have* and *be*. They are used with main verbs to indicate when something occurred (tense): *They have passed their exams.* Some called **modal verbs** express necessity or possibility: *must, should, would, shall, will, can, could, may, might.*

Tense

This indicates when something happens. In the present tense – *plays, is playing, does play,* future tense – *will play, will have played* and past tense – *played, has played, had played.*

8 Perfect punctuation

This chapter explains:

- The way the new punctuation test works.
- The rules that will help you use punctuation correctly.
- How you can use these rules to pass the grammar test successfully.

The new punctuation test was introduced in December 2014 and this section is based on the new tests. Note that there are 15 marks for this test, which is more than for the other literacy tests. You will be expected to punctuate and use capital letters accurately in texts related to teaching.

In the new tests you will not need to delete text but just add punctuation, capital letters and paragraph breaks where necessary. Punctuation is important because you can confuse meaning if you misuse full stops, question marks, commas or other marks of punctuation.

For example: *The pupils like cooking their history lessons and playtime.* The meaning does change if you include a comma after cooking!

Perfect punctuation

The whole point of punctuation is to make certain you convey your meanings clearly and unambiguously to the reader.

Use the diagnostic punctuation test that follows to help you identify any problems you have with using common marks of punctuation. Do this test first and then study the sections where you have made mistakes before completing the final practice test. Hopefully, you will have improved your punctuation skills!

Diagnostic test

This will help you to identify any weaknesses in your ability to use correctly the common marks of punctuation and capital letters. Make certain you study carefully the sections of this chapter which deal with the mistakes you have made.

Read the following sentences/short passages and correct the punctuation mistakes in pencil. If you are uncertain about your answers, please indicate with question marks. The answers are in Appendix 8.1 at the end of this chapter:

1.1 The staff meeting started after school had ended, it finished after the teachers had discussed students planners the end of term disco and the new homework policy.

1.2 The pupils arrived at school with their lunch boxes full of fruit drinks crisps sweets and sandwiches.

1.3 OFSTED inspectors will be in school from tomorrow said the headteacher. Please make certain you arrive at lessons promptly.

1.4 At last you have finished talking said the bad tempered teacher.

1.5 Silence shouted the teacher above the noise of the classroom.

1.6 The boys coats are in the corner and Lauras coat is in the bedroom.

1.7 He came he saw he laughed.

1.8 Are you going to the cinema tonight said Emily to her friends.

1.9 You shouldnt expect Peter to listen if you dont said the teacher to the other pupils in the class.

1.10 the bbc is showing a new version of wuthering heights on friday said the teacher to her sixth-form group.

Sentences

A sentence always begins with a capital letter.

We are going shopping tonight.   Correct

we are going shopping tonight.   Incorrect

A sentence is a number of words that is complete in itself. Typically, it consists of a subject, verb and object.

He (subject) *cooked* (verb) *the meal* (object).

Paragraphs

A paragraph is a group of one or more closely related sentences that develop a central idea. It begins on a new line, which is indented. It is the writer's decision where to begin and end the paragraph. The test might ask you to indicate where new paragraphs should start and end.

Full stops

A full stop is used: to show the end of a sentence, after certain abbreviations, as a decimal point and in internet and email addresses. The vast majority of punctuation marks used in English are full stops and commas.

Perfect punctuation

Commas

If you are not certain about using a comma or full stop then use a full stop and start a new sentence. Commas are not the easiest mark of punctuation to use correctly but should be used in the following circumstances:

(a) To separate words in a list:

Pupils brought books, toys, magazines and sweets to the school summer fayre.

(b) To separate adjectives in a sentence:

The young, charming, innocent teacher faced his class for the first time.

The three adjectives tell you something different about the teacher and you must separate them with a comma. Even if you use only two adjectives you must use a comma to separate them.

The young, charming teacher faced his class for the first time.

(c) After a sentence opener such as:

However
Fortunately
Afterwards
Secondly
Finally

Examples:

Finally, we reached the end of the story.
Afterwards, we all went for a meal.
However, we need to revise the work on atomic theory.

(d) To emphasise something:

For example:

The school hockey team won the cup because their goalkeeper was outstanding.

However, the emphasis but not the meaning would be changed if the sentence read:

Because their goalkeeper was outstanding, the school hockey team won the cup.

(e) Subordinate clauses

Subordinate clauses provide more information about the main sentence:

Stuart, who had always wanted to be a teacher, completed his teacher training course.

Subordinate clauses are not sentences in their own right and need to be marked off from the main sentence with commas. More information about subordinate clauses is given in Chapter 7.

Question marks

These are used to indicate a question and to express doubt or puzzlement, for example:

Can I leave the room? This thought was at the forefront of the pupil's mind.

The question mark comes before the speech marks, for example:

'Can we meet tomorrow?' Mena asked her friends (see below on when to use speech marks).

Brackets

Brackets are used to indicate something the writer would like to add to a sentence as an afterthought or in addition to the main sentence:

I enjoyed teaching (for most of the time) in comprehensive schools.

> *The school has not suspended any pupils this year (as far as I know).*

Speech marks

(a) They identify the words spoken by a person:

You can use either single speech marks (' ') or double speech marks (" "), but try to be consistent in your use of them. You should always use a capital letter for the first word of each sentence inside the speech marks and start a new line for each new speaker in a conversation:

> *"I enjoyed teaching Year 11 today," said Joanne, the PGCE student, to her mentor Laura.*
>
> *"Did John cause any problems?" Laura replied.*
>
> *"No, he was on his best behaviour," Joanne responded.*
>
> *'That makes a change,' said Laura as she left the classroom.*

(b) They are used to surround words which are taken from another source such as a newspaper article or book:

> *The headteacher's report to parents concluded with his target of '75% of Year 11 pupils to achieve five GCSEs at A*–C'.*

Or

> *"Beauty in things exists merely in the mind which contemplates them," wrote David Hume in 1742. This quotation was a favourite saying of the school art teacher.*

Apostrophes

Apostrophes are used to show where letters have been omitted from words (contraction) and also who possesses something (possession).

(a) Contraction:

> I am = *I'm*
> Pick and mix = *Pick 'n' mix*

It is cold = *It's cold*

Did not = *Didn't*

The apostrophe also indicates where numbers have been omitted from a word:

'The Spirit of '45,' was a film made by Ken Loach.

(b) Possession:

(i) To show that a thing or person belongs or relates to something else.

Instead of writing *the party of students* or *the test match of tomorrow,* you can write *the students' party* and *tomorrow's test match.*

(ii) To show possession for singular nouns and most names.

With a singular noun and most personal names, add an apostrophe plus an 's':

I enjoyed Laura's party.

Friday's school trip was cancelled because it rained all day.

(iii) For personal names that end in 's', add an apostrophe plus a further 's'. You would pronounce the extra 's' if you said the word out loud. For example:

He enjoyed Charles's pre-teaching practice party.

Dickens's novels are taught at Key Stage 4 in this school.

(iv) With names that end in 's' but are not spoken with an extra 's', just add an apostrophe after the 's':

The teacher rejected Simon Connors' objections to his essay mark.

The examination board confirmed Susan Towers' grades.

Perfect punctuation

(v) Plural nouns that end in 's'.

Add an apostrophe after the 's':

The girls' school opened in 1968.

Boys' summer PE lessons are athletics and tennis.

(vi) Plural nouns that do not end in's'.

Add an apostrophe plus 's':

The children's books are in their form rooms.

The women's staff room is on the upper floor.

NB: A major problem is the use of *it's*, which is commonly confused with *its*. A way round the problem is to always write *it is* or *it has*:

It's a good idea to revise work on algebra with Year 8.

It is a good idea to revise work on algebra with Year 8.

If you do this you should have no problems using *its* to indicate possession. For example:

Now is the time to give the dog its dinner.

Colons

Used mainly to start a list:

Parents were asked by the headteacher to send their children to school with lots of goods for the school fayre including: books, magazines, biscuits, sweets and soft drinks.

Can also be used to indicate a ratio or proportion. For example:

The teacher/pupil ratio is 1:18.

Used occasionally to introduce a closely related second clause. For example:

He was late for school: the bus had not arrived on time.

Semicolons

The semicolon is rarely used but can be useful in linking independent phrases that are closely related:

> *The school is very good: excellent teachers; an outstanding headteacher; well-behaved pupils.*

It would not be incorrect in this sentence to use commas instead of semicolons.

Exclamation marks

These are used to end sentences where there is an exclamation. For example:

> *Watch that car!*

> *That is not funny!*

Hyphens

Hyphens join words where the meaning of the phrase is closely linked (e.g. *short-term* and *hot-dogs*), but they are not strictly necessary. It is perfectly acceptable to use two separate words.

Capital letters

(a) Are needed at the start of every sentence:

> *The inspectors are in school this week.*

(b) For the names of people and places:

> *Nelson Mandela, Germany, London*

(c) For the titles of people:

> *Queen, Prime Minister, Lord*

Perfect punctuation

(d) For the titles of books, films, organisations:

Sons and Lovers, Star Wars, United Nations

(e) In abbreviations:

BBC (British Broadcasting Corporation)

EU (European Union)

UK (United Kingdom)

Note that every letter should be a capital.

(f) For days of the week and months:

Friday

March

Practice test

The actual test is computerised, but to test yourself on the passages and questions below use a pencil to correct the mistakes and add any punctuation you feel is necessary. Make certain to indicate where you need to start a new paragraph and use capital letters. There are 15 deliberate mistakes in each passage. Answers are at the end of this chapter in Appendix 8.2.

Passage 1

Whenever they meet teachers always talk about pupils, head-teachers homework and holidays. 'Are you watching the bbc tonight. The programme is about secondary schools, is a common remark.

Last friday Mary and jennifer met at the local restaurant to plan their weekend. we could go to the cinema. I think there is a good French film at the Odeon,' Mary suggested. Jennifer was unenthusiastic about this idea and said she would like to wait until Maria arrived

As soon as she said this Maria came into the room and started to complain about pupils in Year 8. The three friends then discussed a number of topics related to school. Mary told Jennifer and Maria that the new curriculum for History would be implemented in the next academic year. It would include the First World War, the French Revolution and the war in Iraq but not the development of Germany from 1930 to 1938. They all agreed that this was a bad idea.

'An OFSTED inspection is likely next year, said Jennifer. We were last inspected a few years ago not as bad an experience as I thought. The headteacher prepared us well for what we needed to do to get a good report. Most of the staff thought the report published in 2011 was a fair assessment of the schools strengths and weaknesses. Mary thought that the inspectors had been very reasonable when making their judgements but Maria thought they had been too critical about book provision in the library.

Passage 2

Dear Parents/Guardians,

As soon as its possible we are planning to take Year 10 pupils on a trip to London. However, it will not be possible to take every pupil we will give pupils on free school meals priority. Teachers are planning many activities these will include visits to the houses of Parliament London Zoo and the National Gallery. More information about this trip will be available next month Speech Night will be held this year on Friday 12th December we hope you can attend. The guest speaker is the director of Education for Botswana. Of course this does not mean that we will concentrate just on africa in Geography next year.

I have been asked by many parents about the new uniform for sixth formers. My Head of Years 12 and 13 Mr D. Johnson, has informed me that the new uniform regulations for the sixth form will include a black dress or trousers;

a school blazer,

a red tie;

black shoes.

I do hope you will be able to continue to support us in providing a quality education for all the pupils at Aire Valley High and you have a good half term break.
Yours Sincerely
Thomas Fisher
Headteacher

For some of you, this chapter will have brought back memories of all those punctuation lessons at school and for some of you it may be the first time that you have seen all the rules that apply when we are using punctuation correctly. It certainly should mean that you can apply these rules to passages that you read and in your own writing. You may even turn into an apostrophe fascist – noticing and correcting all the errors that you will see around you. In fact spotting punctuation errors in the press and in publicity is a great way to continuously revise for this part of the test.

Appendix 8.1

Answers to diagnostic test for punctuation in italics followed by explanations

Question 1.1

The staff meeting start after school had ended. It finished after the teachers had discussed: students' planners, the end of term disco and the new homework policy.

- A full stop is needed after 'ended' because this is a complete sentence in its own right (see section on sentences).

- A capital letter is required for 'It' to start a new sentence (see section on capital letters).

- A colon is used after 'discussed' to introduce a list (see section on colons).

- Apostrophe at the end of 'students' to indicate that more than one student owns the planners (see section on apostrophes).

Question 1.2

The pupils arrived at school with their lunch-boxes full of fruit, drinks, crisps, sweets and sandwiches.

- Commas are used to separate words in the list. It would also be perfectly correct to use a colon after 'of' to introduce the list. You would change the meaning of the list if you deleted the comma between 'fruit' and 'drinks' (see section on commas).

Question 1.3

'OFSTED inspectors will be in school from tomorrow,' said the headteacher. 'Please make certain you arrive at lessons promptly.'

- Speech marks are used to indicate what the headteacher actually said: 'OFSTED inspectors will be in school from tomorrow. Please make certain that you arrive at the lesson promptly.'

Question 1.4

'At last, you have finished talking,' said the bad-tempered teacher.

- Comma after 'last' and speech marks indicating what the teacher said.

Question 1.5

'Silence!' shouted the teacher above the noise of the classroom.

- An exclamation mark needed and speech marks.

Perfect punctuation

Question 1.6

The boys' coats are in the corner and Laura's coat is in the bedroom.

- Apostrophe after the 's' in 'boys' indicates more than one boy and the apostrophe before the 's' in 'Lauras' indicates one person. Remember the apostrophes in these sentences replace the words 'of the'.

Question 1.7

He came; he saw; he laughed.

- Use of the semicolon indicates the close relationship between the three sentences. It would not be incorrect to use full stops instead.

Question 1.8

'Are you going to the cinema tonight?' said Emily to her friends.

- Speech marks are needed and a question mark before the speech mark.

Question 1.9

'You shouldn't expect Peter to listen if you don't,' said the teacher to the other pupils in the class.

- Speech marks needed and two apostrophes to indicate contractions: *shouldn't* and *don't* (should not and could not).

Question 1.10

'The BBC is showing a new version of Wuthering Heights on Friday,' said the teacher to her sixth-form group.

- Capital letters needed for BBC (the name of an organisation), Wuthering Heights (the title of a novel) and Friday (a day of the week).
- Speech marks needed to indicate what the teacher actually said.

Appendix 8.2

The answers to the punctuation tests (both passages)

For both tests the corrections are shown in bold type. The letters following each punctuation mark relate to the explanations at the end of each passage.

Passage 1 with corrections

Whenever they meet teachers always talk about**:** **(a)** pupils, headteachers, **(b)** homework and holidays. 'Are you watching the **BBC** **(c)** tonight**?** **(d)** The programme is about secondary schools,' **(e)** is a common remark.

Last **Friday** **(f)** Mary and **Jennifer** **(g)** met at the local restaurant to plan their weekend. '**We** **(h)** could go to the cinema. I think there is a good French film at the Odeon,' Mary suggested. Jennifer was unenthusiastic about this idea and said she would like to wait until Maria arrived. As soon as she said this Maria came into the room and started to complain about pupils in Year 8. **(i)**

The three friends then discussed a number of topics related to school. Mary told Jennifer and Maria that the new curriculum for History would be implemented in the next academic year. It would include**:** **(j)** the First World War, the French Revolution and the war in Iraq but not the development of Germany from 1930 to 1938. They all agreed this was a bad idea.

'An OFSTED inspection is likely next year,' **(k)** said Jennifer. '**(l)** We were last inspected a few years ago, **(m)** not as bad an experience as I thought. The headteacher prepared us well for what we needed to do to get a good report. Most of the staff thought the report (published in 2011) **(n)** was a fair assessment of the school's **(o)** strengths and weaknesses.' Mary thought that the inspectors had been very reasonable when making their judgements but Maria thought they had been too critical about book provision in the library.

Perfect punctuation

Explanation

a) Colon required to introduce a list.

b) Comma required to separate words in list.

c) Capital letters needed for the name of an organisation.

d) Question mark omitted.

e) Speech marks needed to mark the end of what teachers talk about when they meet.

f) Capital letter needed for a day of the week.

g) Capital letter required for a person's name.

h) Capital letter required for a word starting a sentence.

i) New paragraph required to indicate the change in conversation to school issues.

j) Colon required to introduce a list.

k) Speech marks needed to mark the end of what Jennifer is saying.

l) Speech marks needed to indicate what Jennifer is continuing to say.

m) Comma required to indicate a pause.

n) Brackets used to indicate that this is an aside. They could be replaced with commas.

o) Apostrophe needed before the 's' to replace 'of the'.

Passage 2 with corrections

Dear Parents/Guardians,

As soon as **it's (a)** possible, **(b)** we are planning to take Year 10 pupils on a trip to London. However, it will not be possible to take every pupil. **(c) We (d)** will give pupils on free school meals priority. Teachers are planning many activities. **(e)** These will include visits to: **(f)** the **Houses (g)** of **Parliament, (h)** London Zoo and the National Gallery. More information about this trip will be available next month. **(i)**

Speech Night (j) will be held this year on Friday 12th December. (k) We (l) hope you can attend. The guest speaker is the **Director** (m) of Education for Botswana. Of course, (n) this does not mean we will just concentrate on Africa in Geography next year! (o)

I have been asked by many parents about the new uniform for sixth formers. My Head of Years 12 and 13, (p) Mr D. Johnson, has informed me that the new uniform regulation for the sixth form will include: (q)

a black dress or trousers;

a school blazer; (r)

a red tie;

black shoes.

I do hope you will be able to continue to support us in providing a quality education for all the pupils at Aire Valley High and you have a good **half-term (s)** break.

Yours sincerely, (t)

Thomas Fisher

Headteacher

Explanation

a) An apostrophe needed to indicate a contraction of 'it is'.

b) The subordinate clause appears first and needs to be separated from the main clause with a comma.

c) A full stop is needed to mark the end of a complete sentence.

d) Capital letter at the start of a new sentence.

e) A full stop is needed to mark the end of a complete sentence.

f) Colon required to introduce a list.

g) Capital letter required to indicate the name of a place.

h) Comma required to separate words in a list.

i) A full stop is needed to indicate the end of a complete sentence.

Perfect punctuation

j) A new paragraph required to introduce a new topic, i.e. Speech Night.

k) A full stop is required because this is a complete sentence that is not linked to the next sentence with a conjunction.

l) Capital letter at the start of a new sentence.

m) Capital letter for a person's title.

n) Comma required to indicate that this word is a sentence opener and does not contribute to the meaning of a sentence.

o) An exclamation mark is needed (even though it is a mild exclamation!).

p) Comma required to mark off this phrase, which gives more information about the subject of the sentence, i.e. his name!

q) Colon required to introduce a list.

r) Semicolon to separate items in the list.

s) Hyphen to link these closely related words.

t) The convention about signing letters is a capital letter for *Yours* and small case for *faithfully/sincerely* etc.

9 Comprehending comprehension

This chapter explains:

- The way that the comprehension tests work.
- The important things to remember when responding to a passage.
- The different skills that you will need to pass the tests.

There are 8 to 12 marks for comprehension. This chapter is about understanding and interpreting written material ranging from government documents to reports on developments in teaching and learning.

You will be tested on your ability to:

- identify the key points in a text
- tell fact from opinion
- make inferences from a text and draw deductions
- identify the readership for a text
- read a text and select specified information from it
- evaluate the validity of statements
- complete a list

Comprehending comprehension

- explain the meaning of words and sentences
- select headings for particular sections of the passage.

The questions will test only some of these aspects of comprehension.

This chapter is written slightly differently from the other chapters. I have given you two tests. Try the tests and then use the answers and the explanations in the answers to the tests to help you understand how to respond successfully.

You will be presented with a short text and a series of questions on it. Make certain you read the whole text first before attempting the questions. Remember you may disagree with statements in the extracts but you are NOT giving your own opinions about the matters being discussed.

In the computerised tests you will be expected to drag your answers to the appropriate boxes.

Test 1

Read this extract from an OFSTED document and complete the questions. The passage is from an OFSTED report 'Leading improvements across the system', starting at point 82:

---

82. Good governance is crucial to tackling underperformance and supporting improvement. Governance that is weak does not challenge the school about its performance or press the school to increase its aspirations. Over the past year, inspectors judged governance to be weak and recommended an external review of governance in around 400 schools. Some reviews have now taken place and, in others, action has been taken to replace the governing body with an interim executive board. However, not enough time has passed since all recommendations for review were made for us to judge the impact on the quality of governance overall. We will report on this in greater depth next year.

---

83. There has been a reduction in the proportion of schools judged to require improvement. However, there were still 583 inadequate schools in England at the end of the last academic year, serving 240,000 pupils. Although many schools were removed from a formal category of concern in 2012/13 other schools continue to take their places. Overall, the scale of the problem has not diminished sufficiently.

84. School leaders and governors are primarily responsible for tackling the decline in teaching and standards that usually lead to a school being judged inadequate. But beyond this the responsible authorities, such as local authorities and those that lead multi-academy trusts, have a key role to play.

85. Regular monitoring and early intervention, particularly in English and mathematics, can prevent more widespread failure later. But it must be decisive and linked to high quality support from other schools or organizations. HMI have raised concerns about whether there is sufficient monitoring of, and intervention in, declining schools across the system. In many schools where intervention has taken place, the quality of that intervention has been deficient. As a result, HMI now monitor all schools judged as requires improvement, providing greater challenge with the aim of preventing further decline.

86. In investigating the reasons why 114 of the 480 schools judged inadequate this year failed, HMI identified some of the key leadership features that lay behind the inadequate inspection outcome. In a quarter of the schools, there was a headteacher who had been in post for less than three years, and who had not adapted well to the challenges of their new position. But in another half of schools, the headteacher was long-established or had left the school in the few months prior to it being judged inadequate.

87. Many long-serving headteachers had not updated their understanding of what constitutes effective teaching. Nor had they updated their own skills in monitoring the quality of teaching. Their aspirations for the school and its pupils were usually too low. Many of these long-established heads had not been challenged by their governing bodies. In some cases, the schools had resisted attempts by the local authority, or others, to provide support and challenge.

88. In the failing schools, HMI report the following characteristics:

- governing bodies failed to challenge a well-established incumbent headteacher until it was too late;
- low aspirations arising from a lack of understanding of how good other schools were, and a failure to understand that 'the world had moved on';
- headteachers who failed, for various reasons, to develop their middle and senior leaders;
- schools that were unable to handle the transition to new leadership, either because governors had no plan or there was too little depth in leadership.

89. Last year, we criticised the lack of drive and initiative in some local authorities and began focused inspections in many local areas where school performance had been poor.

Attributing statements to categories

Read the statements below and choose which group each refers to. Put the correct code in the brackets:

Statements

They must take responsibility for tackling underperformance and school improvement. ( )

They need to monitor teaching. ( )

Have raised concerns about monitoring and intervention in poor schools. ( )

Must do more to improve schools which are inadequate. ( )

Groups

Headteachers (HT)

Governors (G)

HMI (H)

Some Local Authorities (LA)

Completing a bulleted list

Re-read paragraph 88. Select three phrases from the list below to make a bullet list of the characteristics of failing schools according to HMI.

( ) number of pupils on free school meals;

( ) weak governing body;

( ) poor headteachers;

( ) low aspirations for pupils;

( ) lack of parental support;

( ) lack of professional development for middle and senior managers;

( ) inadequate discipline;

( ) homework not set regularly.

Matching texts to summaries

From the list of statements below select one that best summarises paragraphs 86 and 87:

( ) The majority of failing schools have headteachers who have been in post for less than 3 years.

( ) Local authorities have not provided enough support to weak headteachers.

( ) Many experienced headteachers have not updated their skills in monitoring teaching and learning.

( ) Governors do not have the skills to hold headteachers to account for improving standards.

Identifying the meaning of words and phrases

From the lists of statements below tick the ones closest in meaning to the quotes in italics:

'Regular monitoring and early intervention, particularly in English and mathematics, can prevent more widespread failure later'

( ) Intervention must be decisive and linked to high-quality support from other schools or organisations.
( ) It must be supported by the governing body.
( ) Parental support is essential.
( ) Schools must evaluate pupils' attainment in English and mathematics and intervene when necessary.
( ) Pupils' expectations must be raised.
( ) Headteachers have to take the lead.

'Good governance is crucial to tackling underperformance'

( ) Governors need to evaluate the quality of teaching and learning in the school.
( ) Governors are the key to ensure pupils achieve their potential.
( ) Governors need to spend more time in school.
( ) Governors need to improve their own skills.
( ) Governors need to evaluate the work of headteachers.

Evaluating statements about a text

Read the statements below and decide whether:

- the statement is supported by the text (s)
- the statement is implied by the text (i)
- there is no evidence concerning the statement (ne)
- the statement is implicitly contradicted by the text (ic)
- the statement is contradicted by the text (x).

Enter the correct letter in the brackets by each statement.

( ) In the majority of failing schools the headteachers have been in post for three years or less.

( ) In failing schools headteachers have not recognised their talented teachers.

( ) Headteachers are out of touch with developments in other schools.

( ) Support from good schools would not help poor schools.

( ) Parents need to play more part in improving standards.

Use of headings

Select and tick the best heading for points 82–89 of this report.

( ) Governors must take the blame

( ) Teachers must do better

( ) Parents blamed

( ) Local Authorities on trial

Identifying the audience

The list below shows possible audiences for points 82–89 of this report. Select the group for which it has the most relevance (MR) and the least relevance (LR).

( ) Parents

( ) Headteachers and governors

( ) Student teachers

( ) Local education authorities

( ) Teachers

Test 2

Read the report below and answer the questions which follow.

Results from the International Student Assessment (PISA) report 2012 for the United Kingdom

Key findings

1   The United Kingdom performs around the average in mathematics and reading and above average in science, compared with the 34 OECD countries that participated in the 2012 PISA assessment of 15-year-olds.

2   When compared with PISA 2006 and PISA 2009, there has been no change in performance in any of the subjects tested. (The PISA 2000 and 2003 samples for the United Kingdom did not meet the PISA response-rate standards, so the observed higher performance in 2000 should not be used for comparisons.)

3   The United Kingdom is listed 26th in mathematics performance, but because results are based on a sample, its relative position could be between 23rd and 31st. Its performance is similar to Czech Republic, Denmark, France, Iceland, Republic of Ireland, Latvia, Luxembourg, New Zealand, Norway and Portugal.

4   The United Kingdom has a higher GDP and spends more on education than the average in OECD countries, as well as higher levels of tertiary education and a lower share of the most socially-economically deprived groups. However, these comparative advantages do not have a clear relationship with educational outcomes.

5   As in many other countries, socio-economically disadvantaged students in the United Kingdom are less likely to succeed at school than their more advantaged peers. However, some countries are more successful than the

---

United Kingdom in reducing the influence of socio-economic status on student performance.

6   On the other hand, students from an immigrant background (first or second generation) in the United Kingdom perform as well in mathematics as other students. This is in contrast to the situation observed in many other OECD countries, where students from an immigrant background score significantly lower.

7   Students in the United Kingdom are generally positive about their experiences at school and about the climate in their classrooms. As in many other countries, they are much less positive about learning mathematics, although students in the United Kingdom are less anxious about mathematics than the average across OECD countries.

8   Girls in the United Kingdom do not enjoy mathematics, are anxious when asked to solve mathematical problems, and underperform compared with boys. Boys also outperform girls in science. Girls outperform boys in reading, although the gap is smaller than in many other countries.

Attributing statements to categories

Read the four statements below. Select the group they refer to and enter the code in the brackets.

Statements

( ) They underperform in mathematics.
( ) They are generally positive about school.
( ) Their performance in mathematics is similar to France, the United Kingdom and Portugal.
( ) Boys' attainment in reading is closer to girls' than in many other countries.

Comprehending comprehension

Groups

Pupils in the UK (UK)
Pupils in Norway (N)
Girls in the UK (GUK)
Boys in the UK (BUK)
Pupils in Germany (G)

Completing a bulleted list

Reread paragraphs 5, 6, 7 and 8. Tick the three bullet points below that show your chosen responses.

The United Kingdom:

( ) spends more on education than other OECD countries
( ) spends more on education than the average in other OECD countries
( ) has more than the average of socially disadvantaged pupils
( ) has immigrant pupils who do as well in mathematics as other groups
( ) is in the top 20 countries for attainment in mathematics
( ) is more successful than other countries in reducing the influence of socio-economic status on student performance
( ) has more boys doing better in science than girls
( ) has more boys doing better than girls at reading.

Presenting the main points

Using the information in the PISA report, tick the four most important priorities for improving school education in the United Kingdom from the list below:

( ) the attainment of socially-disadvantaged pupils
( ) girls' attainment in reading
( ) boys' attainment in reading
( ) boys' attainment in science

( ) girls' attainment in science
( ) the attainment of immigrant pupils in mathematics
( ) girls' attainment in mathematics
( ) boys' attainment in mathematics.

Matching texts to summaries

From the list of four statements below tick the one that best summarises the PISA report:

( ) Pupils in the UK are doing better in science and mathematics than in most other OECD countries.
( ) Pupils in the UK are doing better in science than in most other OECD countries.
( ) Pupils in the UK are more anxious about mathematics than in many other OECD countries.
( ) Standards in UK schools give cause for great concern.

Identifying the meaning of words and phrases

From the list below tick the one that best reflects the meaning of the statement:

> 'These comparative advantages do not have a clear relationship with educational outcomes.' (paragraph 4)

( ) Pupil attainment is not just about how much you spend on education and the number of economically deprived pupils.
( ) There is no connection between spending on education and results.
( ) Pupils do better in countries where less is spent on education.
( ) Pupils enjoy school more in other European countries.
( ) Immigrant pupils do better in other OECD countries.

Evaluating statements about a text

Read each of the statements below about the PISA report and decide which one:

- is supported by the text (s)
- is implied in the text (i)
- has no evidence in the text (ne)
- is implicitly contradicted by the text (ic)
- is explicitly contradicted by the text (c).

( ) The United Kingdom spends less on education than other OECD countries.

( ) In the UK students from immigrant backgrounds do significantly better in mathematics than similar pupils in many other OECD countries.

( ) UK students do better in modern languages than in other OECD countries.

( ) In many OECD countries boys do not read as much as girls.

( ) The UK is not as successful as most countries in improving the attainment of socio-economically disadvantaged pupils.

Use of headings

Tick the heading which would be most appropriate for the first paragraph:

( ) UK girls outperform boys.
( ) UK boys are doing better than girls.
( ) UK pupils do well in science.
( ) UK pupils enjoy school.

Identifying the audience

Put a tick against the most relevant audience for the text and a cross against the least relevant audience.

( ) Pupils
( ) Parents
( ) Headteachers
( ) Teachers
( ) Politicians and decision makers
( ) General public

Answers to Test 1

Attributing statements to categories

Statement

> They must take responsibility for tackling underperformance and school improvement.

Answer – Governors

Paragraph 82 states quite explicitly that *governors* are *crucial* in addressing school improvement. In other words governors cannot ignore issues relating to pupil attainment.

Statement

> They need to monitor teaching.

Answer – Headteachers

Paragraph 87 states that *many long-serving headteachers* have not kept up to date with developments in teaching and have not improved their skills in monitoring the quality of teaching in their schools.

Comprehending comprehension

Statement

Have raised concerns about monitoring and intervention in declining schools.

Answer – OFSTED
Paragraph 89 identifies *OFSTED* has concerns about the effectiveness of the support provided to weak schools in some local authorities.

Statement

Must do more to improve schools which are inadequate.

Answer – some Local Authorities
In paragraph 89 OFSTED comments on the 'lack of drive' in some local authorities where school performance has been poor.

Completing a bulleted list

Bullet list of the three main characteristics of failing schools:

- weak governing body paragraph 82 states that governance was weak in around 400 schools
- poor headteachers paragraph 86 reports that 114 out of 480 schools had inadequate leadership
- low aspirations paragraph 87 comments that many long-established headteachers had low aspirations for their schools and pupils.

Please note
Although *you* may think that lack of parental support, inadequate discipline and homework not set regularly are important factors in whether pupils succeed at school, these are not highlighted in this report. In the PISA report poor teaching is seen as an issue that is not being addressed in failing schools by headteachers. The assumption is that good headteachers will eradicate poor teaching.

Matching texts to summaries

Best statement is:

Many experienced headteachers have not updated their skills in monitoring teaching and learning.

Reasons:

- According to the OFSTED report paragraph 87, it is implicit that good teaching will lead to improved pupil attainment.
- The majority of failing schools have headteachers who have been in post for less than 3 years is contradicted in paragraph 86, which states that in a half of failing schools heads were long established or had recently left the school.
- Local authorities have not provided enough support to weak headteachers. Paragraph 89 does criticise some local authorities, but paragraph 87 says that many schools had resisted attempts by local authorities to help them.
- While governors have a responsibility for holding schools to account for standards, it is the responsibility of headteachers to improve teaching and learning. Paragraph 87 makes this point.

Identifying the meaning of words and phrases

The statement:

Regular monitoring and early intervention, particularly in English and mathematics, can prevent more widespread failure later.

is closest in meaning to:

Intervention must be decisive and linked to high-quality support from other schools or organisations.

Comprehending comprehension

Reason:
It is clear from the passage (paragraph 85) that failing schools on their own will not improve standards. Although governors, headteachers, pupils and parents all have a part to play in improving standards, they will not be able to do this on their own without external support.

The statement:

Good governance is crucial to tackling underperformance.

is closest in meaning to:

Governors are the key to ensure pupils achieve their potential.

Reason:
There is nothing in this passage from the report about the time spent in schools by governors or their own skills. Responsibility for what happens in classrooms lies with the headteacher, who is accountable to the Governors for ensuring children achieve their potential. It is unlikely governors will have the skills to evaluate classroom practice, but they have a responsibility to question the headteacher about standards in the school and to seek external support if necessary.

Evaluating statements about a text

Statement:

In the majority of failing schools the headteachers have been in post for less than 3 years. (x)

No. Paragraph 86 states clearly that although in a quarter of failing schools headteachers have been in post for less than 3 years, this is not the case in the majority of other failing schools.

Statement:

In failing schools headteachers have not recognised their talented teachers. (i)

This is implied in the text because these headteachers have not kept up-to-date with what 'constitutes effective teaching' (paragraph 87).

Statement:

Headteachers are out of touch with developments in other schools. (s)

Yes. Paragraph 88 (bullet point 2) emphasises that these headteachers are not aware of how good other schools are and that 'the world had moved on'.

Statement:

Support from good schools would not help poor schools. (ic)

Inconclusive because paragraph 87 indicates that the headteachers of failing schools are not aware of developments in good schools.

Statement:

Parents need to play more part in improving standards. (ne)

Although this may be true, there is no evidence in this extract from the report.

Use of headings

Governors must take the blame is the best heading for this report because the list does not include headteachers. Some, but not all, local authorities are criticised and although quality of teaching is identified as a major issue the responsibility for improving standards is not just the responsibility of individual teachers. There is no reference to parents, although in many reports on pupil attainment parents/carers are seen as key partners in raising attainment.

Identifying the audience

The most relevant audience is headteachers and governors and the least relevant student teachers. It is clear that OFSTED sees headteachers and governors as the key players in school improvement. The belief is that the quality of teaching will only improve if it is monitored carefully and this is something that is not the responsibility of parents. Local education authorities have a part to play in supporting failing schools but they need the cooperation of governors and headteachers. Student teachers cannot be held responsible for 'failing' schools and will not be placed in them for teaching practice.

Answers to Test 2

Attributing statements to categories

They underperform in mathematics – girls in the UK (GUK) paragraph 8.

They are generally positive about school – pupils in the UK (UK) paragraph 7.

Their performance in mathematics is similar to France, United Kingdom and Portugal – pupils in Norway (N) paragraph 3.

Boys' attainment in reading is closer to girls' than in many other countries – boys in the United Kingdom (BUK) paragraph 8.

Completing a bulleted list

The three bullet points are shown below.

The United Kingdom . . .

* spends more on education than the average in other OECD countries – paragraph 4 makes this point.

- has pupils with an immigrant background who do as well in mathematics as other groups – paragraph 6 states explicitly that this is the case and is in contrast to many other OECD countries.

- has more boys doing better in science than girls – paragraph 8 states that boys in the UK 'outperform girls in science'.

Presenting the main points

Reasons in italics

1   The attainment of socially disadvantaged pupils. *Paragraph 5 stresses that socially disadvantaged pupils in the UK 'are less likely to succeed than their advantaged peers'.*

2   Girls' attainment in mathematics. *Paragraph 8 states that girls in the UK 'underperform compared with boys'.*

3   Girls' attainment in science. *Paragraph 8 states that 'Boys also outperform girls in science'.*

4   Boys' attainment in reading. *Paragraph 8 states that 'girls outperform boys in reading'.*

Matching texts to summaries

The best answer is the second statement in the list because paragraph 2 of the report states that pupils in the UK are doing better in science than in most other OECD countries.

Other responses are wrong because:

- Pupils' attainment in the UK in mathematics is around the average for OECD countries but not above – paragraph 1.

- Pupils in the UK are more anxious about mathematics than in many other OECD countries – contradicted by paragraph 7, which states that they are less anxious than the average across other OECD countries.

- Standards in the UK give cause for great concern is contradicted by paragraph 1, which states that standards are above average in science and average in mathematics and reading.

Identifying the meaning of words and phrases

The meaning of the statement is best reflected by:

Pupil attainment is not just about how much you spend on education and the number of economically deprived pupils. (Paragraph 1)

The other options are incorrect:

There is no connection between the amount of spending and results.

This is too strong a conclusion to draw from the statement – results are not *just* about the amount of spending on education.

Pupils do better in countries where less is spent on education.

There is no evidence that this is the case.

Pupils enjoy school more in other OECD countries than in the UK.

Paragraph 7 states that UK pupils are positive about their experiences at school.

Immigrant pupils do better in mathematics in the OECD than in the UK.

Paragraph 6 states explicitly that these pupils do significantly better in mathematics in the UK than in many other OECD countries.

Evaluating statements about a text

The UK spends less on education than other OECD countries. The answer is (c). In fact paragraph 4 states that the UK spends more on education than the average in other OECD countries.

In the UK students from immigrant backgrounds do significantly better in mathematics than similar pupils in many other OECD countries. The answer is (s). Paragraph 6 indicates that in many OECD countries standards are significantly lower than in the UK.

UK students do better in modern languages than in other OECD countries. The answer is (ne). Although this may be the case there is no evidence in the text to support the statement.

In many OECD countries boys do not read as much as girls. The answer is (i). There is no direct evidence to substantiate this point but it could be inferred from the evidence that because girls' standards in reading across the OECD are higher than that of boys they do, in fact, read more than boys.

The UK is not as successful as most countries in improving the attainment of socio-economically disadvantaged pupils. The answer is (ic). Although some countries are achieving higher standards with socio-economically disadvantaged pupils than in England, this is not the case in many other OECD countries (paragraph 5).

Use of headings

Best heading: UK pupils do well in science
Paragraph 1 states that UK pupils do well in science. There are no references to differences in girls' and boys' attainment or attitudes to school.

Identifying the audience

Most relevant group – Politicians and decision makers
Although this report is of interest to a wide audience, it is intended to inform politicians and decision makers about the state of education in OECD countries and priorities for educational changes.

Least relevant group – Pupils
Although the report is about them, there is little they can do to influence educational changes.

171

Comprehending comprehension

So that completes all the subject knowledge sections. If you have worked through this methodically you should now be at a stage where you can book your test and walk through the test centre doors confident that you will pass.

Your next task is to get that application in and to make sure that you are called for interview.

Read on!

10 Successfully applying for teacher training courses

This chapter explains:

- The qualifications you need to apply for a teacher training course.
- How to choose the course that is right for you.
- The application process for teacher training courses.
- How to write a great personal statement.

Don't read this section until you feel confident in passing the tests. Now you are ready to make an application. This chapter takes you through the application process including choosing the course that is right for you and putting together an outstanding personal statement. Because that is what you need to do – stand out from all the other applicants.

A first port of call for anyone interested in becoming a teacher should be the Department for Education website, https://www. gov.uk/government/organisations/department-for-education. This contains the most up-to-date information; courses change very rapidly. It also contains all the up-to-date links to application forms.

What qualifications do I need?

There are some basic requirements that everyone needs in order to apply for any teacher training course:

GCSEs

To start teacher training you'll need C-grade GCSEs in:

- English
- Mathematics
- A science subject if you want to teach primary or are applying for a Key Stage 2/3 course (ages 7–14).

If you don't have GCSEs in mathematics, English or science, you may be able to take a pre-entry test set by your teacher training provider. You should also check with your provider what they consider to be equivalent to GCSE. You may have completed an access course at a college for example. Some providers accept skills developed through work experience. If you have any concerns, contact the school or the university that you would like to train with to find out exactly what they expect from their applicants.

If you have qualifications from outside Europe, the National Academic Recognition Information Centre (NARIC) will be able to advise you on whether these are equivalent to the minimum requirements set out above. Their website is http://ecctis.co.uk/naric/. Most providers will expect you to carry out this check yourself, so it is important that you do this before making an application.

Degree

Everyone who is awarded Qualified Teacher Status (QTS) must have a degree. Some of you will already have a degree and so will opt for a postgraduate course. These courses normally last a year. You can train to be a teacher following an undergraduate course. These courses usually last three years and you will be awarded a degree as well as QTS at the end of your period of study.

As with GCSE qualifications it is important to check with the provider that you applying to that your degree is appropriate for your course. If your first degree is from outside the European Union you will need to consult with NARIC to check that your degree will be equivalent, as for GCSEs.

School experience

You need to spend as much time as possible in schools before you apply for teacher training. Many of the trainees I teach have spent time as teaching assistants before a successful application and several every year have been unsuccessful on their first application and spend a year working in schools before reapplying and being successful.

The amount of school experience expected varies from one school or university course to another. As a rule of thumb make sure you have at least 10 days' experience before you start your training. Again, check the exact requirements by contacting the providers that you intend to apply to.

Try not to carry out all your school experience in schools that you know well. When I am interviewing prospective trainees I am always more impressed by those people who have put themselves outside their comfort zone rather than spending 10 days in their own school, or the school that their Mum works in. They also tend to have more interesting things to talk about.

What course should I apply for?

The first thing that you need to decide is the age group that you would like to work with. This is not a straightforward decision and I would suggest visiting a range of schools and Early Years settings before you make your decision. This may seem like a long-winded process but it is a very important decision. It also means that when you are asked at interview why you want to teach this particular age group or this particular subject you have a convincing answer.

Some students tell me that they choose to teach younger children because they are worried about their subject knowledge for older children. This answer won't get you a place on a course, I'm afraid; good subject knowledge is vital whatever age you are teaching.

So once you have decided what age group you want to teach or if your passion for a subject is drawing you to a particular subject in secondary school, you can look at the range of courses available.

School-led training

As the title suggests, this means that your training will be predominantly based in a single school. You're selected by the school and based there during your training. All courses will involve some contact with another school because it is important that you experience more than one school during your training. Check carefully with the provider what qualification is awarded at the end of the training. Not all school-based provision awards a Postgraduate Certificate in Education (PGCE) because these can only be awarded by universities.

Some routes that are school led are salaried. For these routes you are employed by the school and receive a salary as you train.

University-led training

Many universities offer teacher training courses for both graduates and undergraduates. Universities work with groups of schools in close partnership to offer at least two school experience placements as part of your training.

Routes for people who are already teaching

If you're already an experienced teacher with a degree but you don't currently have Qualified Teacher Status in England, you may be able to follow the Assessment Only (AO) route. For this route you have to show that you already meet the standards and can therefore be awarded QTS. You can find out more about this route from the Department for Education website. I have taught several teachers who have overseas qualifications or who have taught in International Schools who have successfully followed this route.

What is the application process?

The first thing that you need to do is register with the Department for Education. We suggested earlier that you might use a professional email to register for the skills tests. The same applies here. This email will be used by schools or universities that you apply to and I am always a bit alarmed when I am asked to reply to CheekyTony@ . . . rather than Tony.Cotton@ . . .

References

You need two references for your application. Current requirements for these referees are:

- If you're currently at university, or you got your degree within the last five years, one reference must be from someone at your university who can make comments about your academic ability. This could be a tutor or head of department.

- Your second reference can be from someone who you know from work, or who can provide an insight into your character and potential – but you must not use family or friends as referees.

- If you left university more than five years ago, you can choose two professional referees who can comment on your suitability for teaching.

- If you're applying for a School Direct (salaried) course, one of your references must be from an employer.

These are the current Government guidelines but they make good sense anyway. Your referees need to carry weight with the person that is reading the application, so make sure that you are professional about gaining references. We know your Dad thinks your great – we need to know what somebody more impartial thinks.

The application form

You submit your application through the UCAS website, http://www.ucas.com/apply/teacher-training. It is important to read the details on the site carefully because it is an online application process.

There are two main sections to the form:

Your personal statement: This has to contain no more than 4000 characters (including blank spaces and line breaks). See the examples below to get an idea of what 4000 characters looks like.

Your school and work experience statement: This has a character limit of 1600 (including blank spaces and line breaks).

Writing a personal statement

You must remember that someone will be reading lots and lots of applications. The most important thing is to try to think what makes you different from other applications. What will make the person reading the applications remember you – and for positive reasons.

A good start is describing how you came to the decision that you wanted to teach. Avoid starting with 'I have always known I wanted to teach . . . '; or 'Everyone I know says I will be a great teacher'. Focus on more recent experience and how this has inspired you.

Talk about the qualities that you think you already have which will support you in becoming a teacher.

You should also talk about your previous academic study and how this links to the course you are applying for. Make links between your academic learning and your school experience. How did the things you learned in the classroom apply to the classroom you were working in?

Emphasise your school experience. Avoid just describing it – pick out one or two key incidents that made you 'reflect' on teaching and learning. Everyone will have carried out teaching experience, so just telling the reader that you have had experience won't make you stand out.

It may be worth reflecting on the skills that you think are effective and give examples of which of these you think you have (with evidence of how you know). You may already be an experienced communicator or motivator for example. You may have experience that shows you can be empathetic or deal well with parents.

It is worth reading the educational press or professional journals for an area of teaching you are particularly interested in. It makes a very good impression if you mention an article in the *Times Educational Supplement* that you have read, for example. Maybe it is something that relates to a school you are teaching in. You may be working in a school supporting learners in developing their reading skills, for example, and a research report about reading is mentioned in the press. Similarly you could join a professional organisation if you are applying to a secondary school or if you have a passion for a subject at primary level. You will find these organisations on the web. Examples include the Association of Teachers of Mathematics (ATM), the Association for Science Education (ASE), the National Association for Teachers of English (NATE) and the National Association for Teaching Drama (NaTD).

Don't forget other experiences that will support you in teaching. You may be multilingual – a huge benefit for working in most English classrooms; you may be an experienced sports coach or a talented musician who loves sharing this passion with others. Mention it – this is what makes you unique.

Most importantly spend time on this section of the application. If you rush it you will find yourself being unsuccessful and then you will have another year to perfect it! Read it aloud to yourself; give it people you trust to read through and get honest feedback. And make sure it is grammatically correct and that every word is spelled correctly.

School and work experience statement

This is a separate section on the UCAS Teacher Training form and is distinct from the personal statement. This is where you give details of any previous employment and any school experience that you have, such as teaching assistant work or time you have spent observing in classrooms. You only have 1600 characters for this section.

The key things you need to include are:

- Details of any school that you have spent time in. You should include the name and address of each school as well as the start and end dates and the total time of your work experience.

- Details of any other placements or paid employment, including company names, your role and the start/end dates of your time there. If you have been in paid employment for many years just select the most relevant and explain why you have made this choice.

You need to have at least three years' work experience in any field to apply for the School Direct (salaried) training route, so make sure that this is clear on your application. You should also check with the School Direct Provider that they will see your work experience as relevant.

When you reflect on the relevance of this experience you should discuss what you have learnt from this experience and how it applies to you as a beginning teacher. You will find that you reach the character limit very quickly, so you should go into detail in your personal statement.

Top tips

I asked a group of PGCE students that I am currently teaching what their top tips would be for anyone applying for teacher training. This is a selection from their advice:

'You have to spend loads of time on your application. It gets to be a real pain as you seem to be writing the same thing again and again, but if you rush it is a false economy. Loads of my friends didn't get an interview because they didn't check their application before they put it in. When they reread it they realised there were loads of spelling mistakes and that they hadn't really come across as very interesting.'

'You need to get loads of experience in as many schools as you can. I know people who have been in as agency staff, as learning mentors, as paid or volunteer teaching assistants or even just helping kids read. But, whatever you do, get into schools.'

'I know this sounds silly but you really need to know for sure that teaching is for you. You only find this out by being in a few different schools. I went into a school I hated at first, but when I spent time in a school in the city I realised that this was the sort of school I wanted to work in.'

'You need to make sure that you really get to know the place you are applying to. This is particularly important if you get an interview as you need to convince the people there that you want to come to them and only them.'

Who would you choose?

To close this chapter I have written two contrasting personal statements. While I have written them myself, they are heavily based on applications that I have read. The first represents the vast majority of personal statements that I receive. They say very little about the person that is writing them and these sort of bland statements are very quickly consigned to the 'No' pile. The second is based on an application from my nephew, not for a teaching course but for a 'Physics' course. I have adapted it to fit an application for a teacher training course because it is exactly the sort of personal statement I would want to read. So, thanks Solomon – good advice!

I have annotated both the statements so that you can see what would be going through my mind as I read each one. It is unlikely that I would have got to the end of the first one. Read it carefully though and be as brutal as I am with your own statement. Every single sentence has appeared in applications I have received or is taken from responses to questions in interviews.

Statement A

I have always wanted to be a teacher from a very young **age**. My mum and all of my family always tell me that I am very good with children and I think they are right. I always enjoyed playing at being a teacher and used to line my toys up and take a **register**. This meant that when I was older and started to help out at my Aunties school I knew what teachers were supposed to do. I babysit my nieces and nephews a lot and they like playing with me and always go to

This is a very clumsy sentence and a very poor opening. It certainly doesn't set this applicant apart from the crowd

Again this would put me off straight away. Teaching is not a game to be played with toys. It also shows a very simplistic view of what the role of a teacher is.

bed when they are told. I think this shows that I can get children to do what I want them to do and this should help me as a **teacher**.

Never use babysitting as part of your experience. Babysitting requires very different skills from teaching. Equating the two makes the applicant appear very naive.

Check your apostrophes – this should be Aunty's. Unless you had more than one Aunty working in the school.

I have had lots of experience in school. I helped in my **Aunties** school whenever I could from the age of 11. **Mainley** helping out with after school clubs and sometimes going on schools with the **littlies**. Then when it came to pick a work experience what did I choose – of course it was primary **school**. I am lucky because my mum is a head too and so **i** could work in her school with the teacher that used to teach me. I really enjoyed putting up lots of displays and making the classroom really colourful. I also helped with the reading and sometimes the teacher would let the children read their favourite stories to **me**.

Check your spellings – make sure there are no grammatical or spelling errors in your statement at all. Not a single one!

This is too informal – show that you understand current terminology. Were the children in Key Stage 1 or 2? Which year group?

This would be a good point to describe exactly what you did and, most importantly, what did you learn from it? What excited you and what did you find challenging?

Although working with relatives in school is not the best sort of experience, you can still mention it and explain how it convinced you to follow the vocation of teaching.

Again, too informal.

The 'i' should be an 'I'. Don't use text-speak in the personal statement.

This doesn't sound like there was very much 'teaching', or even observation of teaching, going on. It would be much better to discuss how different the school is now from when you attended it. How has the curriculum changed? What is different about the day-to-day practice in the classroom? These sorts of discussions would show that the applicant had a 'critical eye' and would add a reflective tone which is missing from this statement.

For my degree I studied Psychology. This is obviously very useful for any teacher and I think all teachers should do psychology as part of their **training**. Everything in my degree related to how people learn. Doing a Psychology degree will mean that I already know quite a lot about learning and that will help me be a

The applicant is right. A psychology degree is excellent grounding for a primary teacher. Don't patronise the reader by using 'obviously' though – and don't imply that the degree you studied is the 'best' route into a course.

better **teacher**. My dissertation was about young children and learning and I read the literature and talked to teachers about how young children **learn**.

This point needs expanding. Maybe describe one of the modules that you think has particular relevance to teaching. Or a psychologist that you studied who has important things to say about learning and teaching.

I want to work with Primary age children and probably the younger children as I think they are more fun. I also don't really like numeracy and literacy when they get hard like in Year 6. I am OK at them but **i** wouldn't say they are my best subjects. I think I will be a good teacher for Art and Drama as I am quite a creative person.

This should be a focal point for the application. I am genuinely interested to hear much more. The statement is quite short so there is plenty of space to describe and discuss the dissertation in some depth. This paragraph should tell me that you are capable of study at an advanced level and that you are capable of research in classrooms.

That 'i' again.

For my hobbies I like to do line dancing as it is really good fun and you get to meet lots of interesting people. Maybe I could do things like start a line dancing club at school – I'm sure all the children would like it as much as I do. I am also a good piano player and my mum says that schools always want someone to play the piano in **assembly**.

Too many mentions of 'mum'. And how good a piano player is the applicant? What grade have they studied to. This is a great skill to have, but for so much more than playing in assembly. Again the applicant appears very naive.

Someone once asked me what qualities a good teacher would have. I think they have to be able to make lessons fun, to have a sense of humour and to be quite strict but not over strict. I think all of the time that I have spent in schools shows that I have all of these qualities. I hope that you will ask me to come to interview as I am sure you will find out that i would be really good on your **course**.

This reads as though someone has advised the applicant to add a section on 'qualities'. Again a very naive view of teaching.

Statement B

Physics fascinates **me**. I studied physics at University to better understand the fundamental laws that govern our universe, and build up knowledge of why our universe behaves like it does. I've particularly enjoyed the modules which concern the very large and the very small. Interestingly in my time as a learning mentor I have found that the students I work with, particularly in Year 10 and 11, often share this **fascination**. I am keen to find out ways in which I could build these ideas into classroom practice. This is particularly important in **Key Stage 3** to try and engage more young people with Physics as a discipline. I realise that too few school students go on to study at A level and I would love to be part of a team which inspired young physicians to further their **studies**.

Another area of Physics which fascinates students I work with as a mentor is 'Astrophysics'. They still have youthful desires about becoming astronauts. I have had discussions with them about the more realistic goals of finding out more about black holes. The implausible nature of these objects is what draws students to them I think. My mentees have been interested to find out how they behave and the implications of their existence in areas such as **time**.

I think this is a great opening. Anyone reading this application will be fascinated by Physics too. It is also an unusual way to open an application. This makes it stand out straight away.

This is a clever way to bring in the school experience that will be detailed in the work experience section. It suggests an applicant who has spent a good deal of time in school and who is interested in listening to students.

Good to appear familiar with the terminology around education.

This shows an understanding of current issues in Physics teaching.

This builds on the earlier paragraph and locates the knowledge in classrooms. Suggests that the applicant isn't someone in an 'ivory tower' but someone who enjoys talking about Physics with young people.

Successfully applying

I enjoy reading the science literature. I have just finished 'Smashing Physics' by Jon Butterworth. This details the story of the search for the Higgs Boson at CERN. It gives an insight into being involved with an international research project, and also outlined the physics involved with the experiment. I think it is important to draw on contemporary research in the **classroom**. I understand that the Science and Physics curricula are laid down by government. However I don't believe that teachers should see this as a straitjacket and would endeavour to find ways to show school students that science is relevant **today**. Last year I supported a local school on a trip to the Science Museum in Manchester. The main display discussed the search for the Higgs Boson so I could answer many of the questions that the Year 12 pupils **had**. I know that one of the teachers' standards says that teachers should be able to 'demonstrate a critical understanding of developments in the subject and curriculum areas, and to promote the value of scholarship'. I believe that this experience gives some evidence of my ability to do **this**.

I took part in the Physics Olympiad during my AS year and received a bronze award. During this time I attended lectures at Bradford University, about the existence of antimatter, and at Sheffield University about

Important to show that the applicant is aware of recent developments in the field.

This suggests a pragmatic view of teaching, but tempers this with an enthusiasm that is great to read in any application letter.

Another very useful piece of experience. And something that interviewers would value talking about.

Shows an understanding of current expectations of teachers. And that the applicant has read the teaching standards.

astrobiology. I was also involved in a workshop in Manchester University which gave us an example of the kind of work taking place at the ATLAS experiment. Specifically we looked at particle jets that had been mapped by the detectors in several collisions and looked for the point of collision. I would hope to build the Physics Olympiad into any classroom that I was working in. It may even be something that I could support as part of one of my placements in **school**.

As with previous paragraphs, this develops the view of the applicant as someone with very strong subject knowledge and an understanding of how to apply this to the classroom.

I am very keen to develop a career in physics teaching and would hope to become a Head of Science. The Head of Science at my college allowed me to develop my interest in Physics. It was also noticeable that as many girls as boys studies physics and that one of my physics teachers was a woman. I hope to help break down the myth that physics is just for boys **too**.

More evidence that the candidate has an awareness of current issues and that they want to do something about them!

In my free time I have been a member of Calderdale Theatre School for ten years. This has taken me to the National Theatre in London to perform in the Lyttleton theatre, and also to Glasgow and Lisbon where I worked with international students of drama. These experiences have improved my ability to adapt to environments quickly, and strengthened my communication and teamworking skills. Skills which are vital to **teaching**.

This shows there is more to the applicant than just Physics – and it is related back to teaching again.

Successfully applying

I have valued the chance to share my
experiences with you and very much hope to
be given the opportunity to discuss these
ideas with you further at an interview.

That seems a good place to leave the application process. Hopefully
you have taken on all the advice in this chapter and you will be
offered an interview. Chapter 11 takes you through the interview
in some detail.

11 Acing the interview

This chapter explains:

- What you can expect on an interview day.
- How you can best prepare for the tasks you will be set as a part of the interview process.
- How to plan great answers for the questions that you will be asked.

Great – you read Chapter 10 very carefully and have been asked for an interview. It is a requirement of all teacher training providers that they interview every applicant before they can offer places on the courses that they run. Interview days all follow a very similar process. This chapter will take you through the process step by step so that you can plan to succeed at this final hurdle.

What will happen on interview day?

It is unlikely that the process will simply be a single face-to-face interview. It is very likely that you will be asked to carry out a task that is linked to teaching. You may be asked to observe a piece of teaching and talk about it. You may be asked to work on a problem-solving activity in a group to see how you operate as a member of a team.

It is likely that you will be asked to carry out a task that will assess your literacy skills or other subject knowledge skills. If you are applying for a secondary subject, this will be linked to your subject. If you are applying for a primary course, there may well be additional literacy and numeracy assessments.

The day will end with a face-to-face interview. This is likely to be a member of the team who teaches on the course and a teacher from one of the schools who works with the provider. For school-based programmes the interview will be chaired by someone from the school you will be placed in accompanied by a colleague from the accrediting university.

How can I prepare for the tasks?

The most important thing to do is to find out what sort of tasks the provider who is interviewing you uses. They will send a letter that outlines the process for the day. Read this very carefully. If there is anything that you are uncertain of, ring up and check it out. Nobody will mind you ringing for additional details. In fact it may well be seen as commitment to that course in particular.

Next research the provider carefully. Read all the details on their website. Make notes of things that particularly appeal about their course. It is a great advantage to be able to show you understand what the provider thinks is special about their course. You will certainly be asked why you have applied for this course out of all the courses you could have chosen. You need to have an honest and sincere answer ready. The website is also likely to give details of the interview day.

Reread the earlier chapters in the book, particularly the literacy sections. Many providers will ask you to undertake an additional literacy assessment. For example, one provider I know asks applicants to write on the subject:

A student in one of your classes has returned to school after a period of absence. Not only is he behind in his work, he is also impacting on the behaviour and learners in the group. What strategies would you use to re-engage the learner and ensure that he is able to make good progress in the class?

Or

What or who has inspired you to become a teacher?

Another asks applicants to discuss:

The difference between the roles of Class Teacher and Teaching Assistant.

If you are asked to complete a piece of writing, the assessor will be looking particularly at spelling and grammar, so you need to be extremely careful. Avoid using any words that you are unsure of and keep the punctuation simple. Better to not try and impress with lots of colons and semicolons than use them inappropriately. Avoid generalisations too: do not say things like 'Everyone knows . . . ' or 'Most students don't like homework'. Only put forward arguments that you can support. It is better to draw directly on your experience and offer any opinions tentatively.

You also need to make sure that your subject knowledge in mathematics, and your secondary subject if applying for secondary subject, is up to date so that you can respond confidently to any questions. Maybe have another go at the practice numeracy and literacy tests before the day as a means of revising.

If you are asked to work in a group on a task or to take part in a group discussion, think carefully about any contribution you make. A colleague once told me that they try to make only three contributions to any discussion. This means that they think very carefully about the points that they make. I think this is a good rule of thumb. If you make three pertinent points you will be noticed for the right reasons. If you talk too much the assessor may think that you are 'too pushy'; if you say nothing you won't be noticed at all.

If you are asked to observe a classroom, focus on the positive things that you notice. Observe one or two of the children so that you can describe moments when you saw some learning take place. If you can, support this with evidence. Describe something that a pupil said in response to a teacher's question, or something interesting that a pupil wrote in their book. Alternatively watch the teacher and make notes on particularly effective parts of their practice that you can describe. Talk about how you know that these aspects of their practice were effective. Remember, it is likely that the person who is interviewing knows the teacher you observed and works with the pupils. So, whatever you do, don't be negative.

What will I be asked in my interview?

The interviewing team will be listening to your answers to give them evidence of your qualities. You should therefore try to tailor your answers and contributions to reflect the qualities they are looking for in a teacher. They are likely to include:

- Evidence of your commitment to teaching. This will probably include looking for a realistic but positive view of the role.
- An understanding of the qualities that make up a 'good' teacher.
- An enthusiasm for your subject and evidence of good subject knowledge.
- An awareness of current big issues in education.
- Excellent personal skills and good communication skills.
- A positive attitude towards children and working with children.
- An ability to communicate in accurate spoken English.

How should I prepare?

Of course the key to success is preparing well. You will have already researched the course and institution you're interviewing for thoroughly, so you will know the qualities that they value. Make a note of these and jot down the evidence that you have these qualities.

You can research the issues surrounding education and teaching in general by reading the *Times Educational Supplement* or an appropriate subject association journal. Select a couple of articles that interest you and write a brief summary so that you can discuss the key issues if they come up in the interview.

Reread your personal statement so that you can confidently talk about your reasons for applying for this course in particular and your driving force in becoming a teacher. It is very likely that you will be asked about your experience in school, so make sure that you can speak with authority about this in the interview.

The next step is to look at the section below and jot down how you might respond if asked these questions.

What questions might I be asked?

You will almost certainly be asked to explain why you want to become a teacher. You need to convince the interviewers that you are genuinely excited by the prospect of working with young people. You will need to persuade them that you have a passion to support learners to develop skills and understanding in your chosen subject or across the curriculum if you are applying for a primary course. Draw on your experience in schools to give a convincing answer.

Most interviews also include a question exploring the *qualities you think make a good teacher.* List the qualities for yourself; it is important that you do not just reproduce a list that someone else has given you. A good way to respond to this answer is to think of a teacher who has inspired you. Think about, and talk about, the qualities that they had and why you think they are important for all learners. There is likely to be a follow-up question that asks which of these qualities you think you already possess. This is where you can draw on your experience to describe times when you felt you were exhibiting these skills. Try to balance confidence in some areas with ways in which you will work at those qualities you still need to develop.

There will be a question that is designed to explore your analytical and reflective qualities. You may be asked, for example, about the *main differences between education today and in your own time in school.* Again you should draw on your own experience so that the answer is personalised. Differences are likely to include the curriculum. This gives you an opening to talk about your understanding of the current curriculum, which you will have researched before the interview. It is also very probable that the classrooms you have worked in used technology in a greater range of subjects and in very different ways than it was used when you were a learner. Try to focus on positives here. Don't generalise and talk about how much worse the behaviour is or how attendance is a bigger problem 'these days'. First, this is a crass generalisation and, second, it is not true.

You will certainly be asked about *your subject knowledge and how you think your recent academic study will support you in becoming a teacher.* Your research of the curriculum will allow you to make links between your studies and the current curriculum. There will be areas of the curriculum that you are less certain about. This is absolutely fine. If you can identify these areas and talk about how you will develop your knowledge in these areas, it will be seen as a strength.

Interview panels will want to check that you are up-to-date on current issues in teaching and will certainly ask for *your opinion on current educational issues.* This is another area in which it is important to have your own opinion based on your reading of the educational press. From the moment you begin the application process you should be reading the *Times Educational Supplement* and subject association journals. If you make notes on one story every week, you will have a wide range to draw on by the time you get to your interview. You will also be able to describe how issues develop and are responded to, because you will have read about them over time rather than simply parroting the latest headline.

It is likely that the panel will ask about your *approach and thoughts about equality issues*. Experience in a wide range of schools is important for many reasons. Coming to an understanding of the importance of diversity is one of the reasons that working with learners from all backgrounds will help you. If you do not have this breadth of experience, make sure this is an area that you read about so that at least you can talk about the issue knowledgeably. Find out the current statistics about attainment – it is likely that certain groups of learners underachieve in some areas. You could find out success stories in these areas, which you could share at interview.

The final question usually asks you to describe *other skills and interests that you have which will be of value to you as a teacher*. Prepare carefully for this answer. Think back through your experience and about how your other areas of interest have supported you. Your experience in work may have helped you develop communication skills with adults, even mediating skills with angry customers. You may have work experience that involves you working closely with others. You may have interests in theatre, art, music, sport that you could draw on in school. Whatever you do, talk about something: the interviewers are looking for someone interesting, and someone who can engage learners outside the formal curriculum as well as subject specialists. Think about the letter at the end of the previous chapter. Didn't you feel the applicant 'come alive' when they described their time in theatre school, even though they were a physicist?

Most interviewers will be completing a pro forma during the interview. They may even be grading you on the answers that you give so that they can compare you to other candidates on the day. Don't be thrown by this. Try not to let it put you off. It can be disconcerting to see someone writing something just after a question. You will start to think, 'What did I say? Was that a good answer or a bad answer?' Try to ignore these voices in your head and just focus on the answers you are giving. After all, you have prepared carefully. What could go wrong?

This is an example of a proforma that is used by a local provider that I work closely with. A good way to prepare is to write the questions down on separate pieces of paper and ask a friend to select the questions at random. To make it even more realistic, ask them to jot down a few notes while you are speaking. They can then help you afterwards by being honest with you. Which answers came over as most convincing? Which answers did you appear uncertain about?

Then go back over your answers and think of other things that you could have said. Much better to have this happen before the interview!

Question	Comments	Grade
1. Introduce yourself to us – describe your professional journey and why you want to join the teaching profession. *Follow-up: What is it about you as an individual/your personality that would make you a great teacher?* *Why have you applied for this course in particular?*		
2. Give us an example of when you have worked effectively in a team? *Follow-up: If your team hasn't been effective, what did you do?*		
3. What has been your greatest challenge to date? *Follow-up: How will you use this experience to enable you to become an effective teacher?*		

Question	Comments	Grade
4. From your experience working with children, what have you learned about what makes a good lesson and what do you think makes an effective learning experience? *Follow-up: Can you think of an example of amazing learning that you have been part of?*		
5. What inspired you to teach your subject/phase, and how would you enthuse the learners in your classes? *Follow-up: From your time observing in the classroom here, what do you think young children need to learn and develop?*		
6. Trainees have to teach the full primary curriculum (or You have chosen to teach SUBJECT) Tell us about . . . (a) your strengths (b) areas for development in relation to the curriculum.		
7. We have asked you to bring an artefact/resource – you have three minutes to describe what you have brought, why you have brought it, and how you would use it in a teaching context. *Follow-up: What does it tell us about you as a teacher?*		

Acing the interview

Question	Comments	Grade
8. What qualities would you expect an outstanding or high-impact teacher to exhibit? *Follow-up: How will you try to make sure that every student in your class makes at least good progress given their starting points?*		
9. Schools work hard to develop good relationships with the learners. How do you define an appropriate teacher staff/pupil relationship? (Safeguarding question) *Follow-up: If a student asked you to keep something confidential, what would your response be?*		
10. Can you tell us why thinking about equality and diversity are important for schools?		
11. What do you think is the most important issue in education at the moment? *Follow-up: What do you read to keep up to date with developments in education?*		
12. Is there anything else you would like to share with us?		

So, that's it. Good luck in the interview and then enjoy a wonderful career as a teacher. And if either Dave or I bump into you on your course or in the classroom, say hello and tell us what we could have done to make this book even better.

Index

Index